Depression
and the Soul

Depression and the Soul

A Guide to Spiritually Integrated Treatment

John R. Peteet

Routledge
Taylor & Francis Group
New York   London

Routledge
Taylor & Francis Group
270 Madison Avenue
New York, NY 10016

Routledge
Taylor & Francis Group
27 Church Road
Hove, East Sussex BN3 2FA

© 2010 by Taylor and Francis Group, LLC
Routledge is an imprint of Taylor & Francis Group, an Informa business

Printed in the United States of America on acid-free paper
10 9 8 7 6 5 4 3 2 1

International Standard Book Number: 978-0-415-87895-1 (Hardback)

For permission to photocopy or use material electronically from this work, please access www.copyright.com (http://www.copyright.com/) or contact the Copyright Clearance Center, Inc. (CCC), 222 Rosewood Drive, Danvers, MA 01923, 978-750-8400. CCC is a not-for-profit organization that provides licenses and registration for a variety of users. For organizations that have been granted a photocopy license by the CCC, a separate system of payment has been arranged.

Trademark Notice: Product or corporate names may be trademarks or registered trademarks, and are used only for identification and explanation without intent to infringe.

Library of Congress Cataloging-in-Publication Data

Peteet, John R., 1947-
    Depression and the soul : a guide to spiritually integrated treatment / by John R. Peteet.
        p. cm.
    Includes bibliographical references and index.
    ISBN 978-0-415-87895-1 (hardback : alk. paper)
    1. Depression, Mental. 2. Spirituality. I. Title.

RC537.P437 2010
616.85'27--dc22
                          2010007098

Visit the Taylor & Francis Web site at
http://www.taylorandfrancis.com

and the Routledge Web site at
http://www.routledgementalhealth.com

Contents

Acknowledgments / vii
Introduction / ix
1 Heart, Mind, and Soul / 1
2 Depression and Spirituality / 29
3 Differential Diagnosis, Assessment, and Formulation / 71
4 Integrated Treatment / 111
5 Suicide / 149
6 Models of Care / 169
7 The Brain, Depression, and Spirituality / 185
Index / 199

Acknowledgments

Many individuals contributed directly or indirectly to the preparation of this manuscript. I am especially grateful for the careful reviews and thoughtful comments of Kristine Lima, Ruth Redington, Sam Thielman, and Gwyneth Lewis.

Contact Information:

John R. Peteet, M.D.
Department of Psychiatry
Brigham and Women's Hospital
75 Francis Street
Boston, MA 02115

Associate Professor of Psychiatry
Harvard Medical School

Phone (617) 278-0438
Fax (617) 632-6180
E-mail: jpeteet@partners.org

Introduction

Depression is among the most common human afflictions. Almost 12 percent of Americans report two or more depressive symptoms[*] and depression is the leading cause of disability worldwide.[†]

Efforts to raise public awareness of both depression and advances in neurobiology have contributed to greater use of psychopharmacologic treatments. As antidepressants have become the most prescribed class of medications, the percentage of individuals who are also treated with psychotherapy has declined.[‡]

Yet depression is clearly multidimensional. Much depressive suffering results from the way that it permeates the whole self—the way that one thinks, feels, and experiences the world. Sufferers tend to feel not only personally unhappy, but that the world is oppressive, that life is meaningless, and that God

---

[*] Judd et al. (1994).
[†] WHO (2009).
[‡] Olfson et al. (2009).

is disapproving. Something seems wrong with the soul—the core, or essence of who one is. Because depression can so closely resemble ordinary spiritual experience, many religious individuals resist treatment because they feel they should simply have more faith. Religious communities sometimes regard depression as an illness, and sometimes as evidence of spiritual weakness, or even as a punishment.

Mental health professionals often hesitate to address the spiritual dimension of their patients' experience for several reasons. Some view spirituality as an epiphenomenon of more basic neurobiological processes and, as such, of only peripheral interest to psychiatry. Others regard religion as a potentially harmful, immature form of wish fulfillment. Still others have ethical concerns about charging patients and their insurance companies for spiritually oriented interventions, or about influencing patients on the basis of their own personal values. Many lack sufficient familiarity with their patients' spiritual traditions or experience to collaborate effectively with religious professionals, or retain unresolved conflicts in their own relationship with spiritual authorities.

All of these reasons point to the need for a broadly accepted conceptual framework for approaching the spiritual dimension of depressive conditions. In the chapters that follow, I offer a possible framework and describe its practical implications for treatment. Clinical vignettes used for illustration represent actual, disguised cases drawn primarily from my own practice.

In Chapter 1, I attempt to better define the extent of a clinician's role in dealing with spiritual concerns by reexamining the concept of mental health. How can clinicians promote and preserve fully adaptive or healthy functioning? I suggest that full functioning of a person's core, or essential self (one's soul, in Aristotle's sense of key embodied capacities), involves relating to a larger context—the "horizon of significance" which, as Taylor[*] explains, defines authenticity. Specifically, I consider how spirituality grounds the self in various domains of existential concern, such as identity, hope, meaning, morality, and connection. I also consider how spirituality can be harmful or problematic, and respond to some objections to my conclusion that the health of the heart, mind, and soul are clinically important, intimately related, and yet distinct.

In Chapter 2, I explore the complex relationship between depression and spirituality. What does epidemiologic and other research evidence have to teach us? What are the existential struggles of depressed individuals in the areas of identity, hope, and meaning? What perspectives do various traditions of belief offer? How can spirituality help and worsen depression? In what ways can depression both enhance and undermine spirituality?

In Chapter 3, I discuss the differential diagnosis, assessment, and case formulation of depressive disorders, including their spiritual dimension. These include melancholic, bipolar,

---

[*] Taylor (1991).

and psychotic depression; depression associated with personality disorder, addiction, and trauma; adjustment disorder; complicated grief; demoralization; angst; guilt; the "dark night of the soul"; ordinary unhappiness; and the spiritual complications of depression. I then suggest ways that clinicians can screen for, assess, and more deeply explore both spiritual distress and potential spiritual resources, so as to incorporate them into the clinical formulation.

In Chapter 4, I outline an approach to comprehensive treatment. How does an understanding of the patient's emotional needs and existential concerns inform the goals of the work? When are spiritually oriented interventions (for example, cognitive behavioral, humanistic, or interpersonal) indicated? How can a clinician use these to address depressive vulnerabilities such as problems related to perfectionism, negative self-identity, or self-sacrifice? What special boundary, role, and transference considerations does spiritually integrated treatment present?

In Chapter 5, I examine the spiritual aspects of suicide. How do religion and spirituality influence the likelihood of suicide? How can clinicians take this evidence into account in assessing and reducing risk? What spiritual resources can they help suicidal individuals bring to bear in their struggles with self-worth, hope, guilt, and isolation? What helps families and friends to heal in the aftermath of a completed suicide?

In Chapter 6, I compare various models for providing spiritually integrated care within secular and faith-based settings.

What should be the minimal level of spiritual care? What opportunities for providing integrated care exist for pastors, pastoral counselors, therapists, and religiously and spiritually oriented group programs? What are the limitations of models centered on each of these? How can clinicians and spiritual professionals collaborate and learn from each other, so as to effectively address the clinically relevant spiritual needs of depressed individuals?

Finally, in Chapter 7, I consider the implications of advances in neurobiology and psychopharmacology. What do we know about the neurobiological substrates for mood and spiritual experience, and about their significance? Does a "chemical imbalance" preclude a spiritual approach to depression? What are the moral and spiritual implications of using medication to reduce sensitivity to the world's pain?

In "the age of the brain," the mind can appear less important, and the soul even less. I hope to show here what a spiritual perspective can contribute to understanding how depression erodes a sufferer's sense of worth, hope, purpose, or connection, and how a clinician can facilitate that sufferer's return to full health.

References

Judd, L.L., Rapaport, M.H., Paulus, L.P., & Brown, J.L. (1994). Subsyndromal symptomatic depression: A new mood disorder? *J Clinical Psychiatry,* 55 Suppl., 18–28.

Olfson, M., & Marcus, S.C. (2009). National patterns in antidepressant medication treatment. *Arch Gen Psychiatry,* 66, 848–856.

Taylor, C. (1991). *The Ethics of Authenticity*. Cambridge, MA: Harvard University Press, pp. 31–41.
World Health Organization. (2009). *Depression.* http://www.who.int/mental_health/management/depression/definition/en/; accessed August 15, 2009.

1 Heart, Mind, and Soul

The best physician is also a philosopher.

Galen

When is guilt pathological? Should full health be a goal of treatment for depression? How should a clinician approach a patient who feels his life is pointless?

Answering such questions requires a frame of reference for understanding health which is larger than the checklist of symptoms that have often come to define depression. Many if not most clinicians choose a framework based on adaptive functioning in the world. But as Vaillant[*] points out, assessing functional adaptation depends on understanding the tasks of living.

Thinking clearly about what it means to live successfully, or to flourish, has at least three practical benefits: it provides clinicians with tools for distinguishing normal from abnormal.[†] It helps

---

[*] Vaillant et al. (1977).

[†] Havens (1984).

them recognize problems that need attention before they reach clinical significance. And it provides ways to identify and enlist patients' strengths and resources on their behalf. Recognizing this, the recovery movement,[*] informed by the findings of positive psychology,[†] has recently challenged psychiatry to balance its traditional emphasis on pathology with an appreciation of individuals' strengths, growth, positive emotions, and character traits.[‡] Responding by endorsing the concept of recovery, the American Psychiatric Association has agreed that:

> ... the best results come when patients feel that treatment decisions are made in ways that suit their cultural, spiritual, and personal ideals. It [the concept of recovery] focuses on wellness and resilience and encourages patients to participate actively in their care, particularly by enabling them to help define the goals of psychopharmacologic and psychosocial treatments.[§]

In order to examine in subsequent chapters the ways that depression impairs full functioning and the ways that clinicians can help to restore it, in this chapter I briefly review current concepts of successful living relative to the heart (emotion and volition), the mind (cognition and coping), and the soul (the self in relation to transcendent reality). Although not the primary focus here, these of course all depend on the function of the body (the brain, discussed further in Chapter 7). My conclusion is that all

---

[*] Liberman (2005).
[†] Carr (2004).
[‡] Lukoff (2007).
[§] American Psychiatric Association (2005).

these conceptions are consistent with the importance of the heart and soul to human flourishing.

The Heart

Despite its lack of explicit focus on emotional health, and what might at first appear to be psychiatry's suspicion of emotion and neglect of the will, both neurobiology and the actual goals of the major therapeutic schools highlight the importance of emotion and volition.

From a neurobiological perspective, emotions generated in the limbic system normally serve alerting, protective, and motivating functions. Mobilizing to fight, to flee, or to mate ensures survival. Severely depressed individuals often lose this self-protective ability and, at times, even the will to survive.

Freud focused on the elemental, almost instinctual nature of self-protective emotions in formulating the structural theory of the mind.[*] According to his model, libidinous drives or wishes represented by the id push for satisfaction against the constraints of the superego. The resulting tension, mediated by the ego, can lead to "aim-inhibited," or sublimated emotional investment in relationships, activities, or ideals. Despite revisions to Freud's theory, the concept of libido as emotional energy remains important clinically, and its use to denote sexual interest is important in assessing depression. Anhedonia, the lack of ability to enjoy

---
[*] Freud (1923).

usually invested ("cathected," in psychoanalytic terms) activities is a cardinal feature of depression.

Freud also saw distressing emotions indicating the presence of unresolved, unconscious conflict (for example, over a forbidden wish or an unacknowledged loss). While neurotic anxiety or depression serves a signaling function, a severely depressed, overwhelmed individual might lose the capacity to recognize the existence of a more basic problem.

Freud famously advocated rational insight into and control of the emotions: "Where Id was, there ego shall be." In practice, psychoanalytic psychotherapy attends to affect as the path to truth about internal conflicts, calls for the therapist to resonate with the patient's emotional experience, and stresses the mutative potential of a "corrective emotional experience." A successful treatment, as Roy Schafer[*] points out, helps the patient to work through feelings of humiliation, mortification, envy, or disappointment that have made for a joyless life.

Similarly, Freud's emphasis on the childhood origins of psychic conflict and on the unconscious mechanisms by which they operate could seem to imply a kind of psychic determinism that would invalidate the will. Yet a central objective of dynamically oriented psychotherapy is to enhance the individual's capacity to choose freely. Ainslie[†] has recently reviewed

---

[*] Schafer (2003).

[†] Ainslie (2005).

the factors, including emotion and a motivated unconscious, that influence healthy will.

Existential psychotherapists such as Farber,[*] May,[†] and Yalom[‡] have also focused on willing as central to effectively confronting the human condition. They remind clinicians of the importance of consciously facing the threatening concerns of death, freedom, isolation, and meaninglessness. "Learning to live well is to learn to die well; and conversely, learning to die well is to learn to live well" (Yalom, p. 30). Farber[§] distinguishes two realms of the will, one that moves in a direction and the other that moves toward a particular object. However, he recognizes that not all important objectives can be willed:

> I can will knowledge, but not wisdom; going to bed, but not sleeping; eating, but not hunger; meekness, but not humility; scrupulosity, but not virtue; self-assertion or bravado, but not courage; lust, but not love; commiseration, but not sympathy; congratulations, but not admiration; religiosity, but not faith; reading, but not understanding. (p. 15)

For May,[¶] the answer to this problem is that love needs to complement will: "in the long run, love and will are present in each genuine act."

Cognitive behavioral therapy (CBT) seems at first to suggest that feeling is secondary to thinking, by pointing out that how

---

[*] Farber (1966).
[†] May (1969).
[‡] Yalom (1980).
[§] Farber (1966).
[¶] May (1969).

people feel is influenced by how they think. Yet the goal of CBT is to free the patient from the tyranny of automatic and irrational thoughts—not to suppress, or minimize the importance of emotion. Mindfulness as a goal of CBT involves reflection, attunement, and an openness to feelings that makes for greater flexibility and resilience.[*]

Acceptance and commitment therapy (ACT), a more recent form of behavioral treatment, frames the core problem in many forms of psychopathology as "experiential avoidance." As Hayes et al.[†] point out, experiential avoidance "occurs when a person is unwilling to remain in contact with unwanted private experiences (e.g., thoughts, feelings, memories, bodily sensations) and takes steps to alter the form or frequency of these events and the contexts that occasion them despite a significant functional cost caused by this avoidance." Treatment aims to redirect the patient's efforts to more workable solutions by enhancing willingness to experience feelings such as anxiety, by generating defining values and by fostering committed action. Again emotion and will are central to healthy functioning.

Interpersonal therapy (IPT) focuses on the importance of relationships that have the greatest emotional valence for an individual, exploring in each session the links between interpersonal events and mood.[‡] Studies have shown efficacy in depression

---

[*] Siegel (2007).

[†] Hayes et al. (1999).

[‡] Weissman et al. (2000).

when individuals learn to grieve and deal better with other interpersonal problem areas.

Finally, positive psychology regards the capacity to experience positive emotions such as joy and love as fundamental to optimal well-being. As one of its leading figures Martin Seligman[*] puts it, positive psychologists do not claim to have invented the good life or to have ushered in its scientific study, but have attempted to unite under the term *positive psychology* what had been scattered and disparate lines of theory and research about what makes life worth living. For example, Fredrickson[†] posits a broaden-and-build theory according to which "experiences of positive emotions broaden people's momentary thought—action repertoires, which in turn serves to build their enduring personal resources, ranging from physical and intellectual resources to social and psychological resources." Fredrickson[†] and Seligman et al.[‡] have recently presented empirical support for this approach.

The goals of the major therapeutic schools then suggest a central role for the integrated action of emotion and will in healthy human functioning. More specifically, satisfying relationships depend on positive emotions and on character strengths such as kindness, authenticity, and gratitude. The values that shape these character strengths express one's ultimate commitments. In this way, the health of the heart depends on the health of the soul.

---

[*] Seligman et al. (2005).

[†] Fredrickson (2001).

[‡] Seligman et al. (2005).

The Mind

Several conceptions of mental health highlight coping and cognition. George Vaillant, who for decades led the Harvard Study of Adult Development, has distinguished six models of positive mental health.[*] The first model, being "above normal," is represented by axis V of the DSM-IV,[†] the Global Assessment of Functioning (GAF). High scores on the GAF reflect "superior functioning in a wide range of activities, life's problems never seem to get out of hand, is sought out by others because of his or her many positive qualities." A second model based on positive psychology emphasizes love, temperance, wisdom and knowledge, courage, justice, and transcendence. A third model stresses maturity, as evidenced by achieving Erikson's developmental tasks of identity, intimacy, generativity, and integrity. The fourth model calls attention to the importance of social and emotional intelligence, or the ability to read others' emotions. The fifth model defines mental health as subjective well-being, which appears to depend as much on temperament as on environment. And the sixth emphasizes resilience, or adaptable means of coping.

A seventh, more broadly based model than Vaillant's six, can be constructed from the integrated achievement of ideals represented by various complementary paradigms. Havens

---

[*] Vaillant (2003).
[†] American Psychiatric Association (1994).

in his pioneering book *Approaches to the Mind: Movement of the Psychiatric Schools from Sect Toward Science*[*] compared the objective-descriptive, psychoanalytic, interpersonal (social), and existential. Lazare, in his paper of the same year[†] on hidden conceptual models in clinical psychiatry, similarly distinguished the medical, the psychologic, the behavioral, and the social. In 1978, George Engel[‡] called for clinicians to adopt a biopsychosocial approach. The interpersonal or social paradigm that they present has since been elaborated further by feminist, interpersonal, and family therapists. In 1983 (and in a second edition, 1998) McHugh and Slavney[§] advocated for the simultaneous use of four perspectives on the patient: the disease, dimensional, motivated behavior, and life-story (narrative). More recently, a number of clinicians in psychiatry, nursing, social work, and palliative care[¶,**] have called for updating Engel's approach to a biopsychosocial spiritual one, in recognition of the importance to patients of spiritual needs.

These seven models differ in the methods they suggest for measuring mental health, but they overlap with one another and with prevailing conceptions of health to a striking degree: Optimal human functioning by any standard reflects

---

[*] Havens (1973).
[†] Lazare (1973).
[‡] Engle (1978).
[§] McHugh and Slavney (1998).
[¶] Sulmasy (2002).
[**] Ben-Arye et al. (2006).

the effective integration of emotion and cognition within a context of relationships, directed toward realizing the value commitments that order these relationships. Healthy relationships with the self involve value commitments to self-care or self-regard; healthy relationships with others involve value commitments to altruism, empathy, or forgiveness. As existential and biopsychosocial spiritual approaches emphasize, these value commitments are grounded in a larger context of meaning, linking them inextricably with the health of the soul.

But what of the ways that people value certain aspects of mental health differently? Whether one prioritizes love, autonomy, courage, efficiency, and so forth, depends on his world view, or particular framework of ultimate meaning. In this sense too the soul is integral to what each person regards as mental and emotional health.

The Soul

The past few decades have seen a burgeoning of interest in the relationship between spirituality, religion, and health. Freud's antireligious interpretations of faith have been succeeded by more nuanced explorations of its dynamic significance by object relations theorists such as William Meissner and Ana-Maria Rizzuto. Clinical psychologists including Richard Bergin and Allan Richards have published books on various forms of spiritually oriented psychotherapy, including mindfulness. Respect for the diversity of patients' cultural and religious beliefs has become part of cultural competence, and educational programs in medical schools and residency training programs have proliferated, many supported by the John Templeton Foundation. Many of these include instruction on how to assess a patient's spiritual needs. Recently psychiatrists have called attention to the clinical importance of both the therapist's and the patient's world view. Consistent with this, Curlin et al.[*] in 2005 published a survey of over 1000 U.S. physicians, 55 percent of whom responded that their religious beliefs influence their practice of medicine.

The World Psychiatric Association's Section on Religion, Spirituality and Psychiatry has proposed a draft position statement on religion and spirituality in psychiatry that reads in part,

> ... spirituality and religion are concerned with the core beliefs, values and experiences of human beings. A consideration of their relevance to the origins, understanding and treatment of psychiatric disorders should therefore be a central part of clinical and academic psychiatry. Spiritual and religious considerations also have important ethical implications for the clinical practice of psychiatry. In particular, it is affirmed here that:
>
> 1. Spiritual well-being, as indicated in the WHO definition of health, is an important aspect of health... (Verhagen, personal communication, 2008)

---

[*] Curlin et al. (2005).

Yet spirituality remains difficult to define clearly.[*,†] As a result, individuals have often approached spirituality as the proverbial blind men explored the elephant, each using his/her own favored paradigm. A religious believer may approach spirituality as a window into a supernatural realm; an atheist as a psychological phenomenon in principle understandable in naturalistic terms; a sociologist as an aspect of cultural diversity; a psychologist as a means of coping; an existentialist as a way of finding meaning; and the open-minded agnostic as mystery. This lack of agreement on an operational definition of spirituality has made it difficult to discuss the relationship between mental and spiritual health.

The remainder of this chapter briefly examines recent attempts to define spiritual health, suggests a different model that sees spiritual and mental health as distinct but directly related, and considers possible objections to acceptance of this model.

Generally, the term religion denotes a tradition of beliefs and practices shared by a community, whereas spirituality is a broader category that refers to a person's connection with a larger or transcendent reality that gives life meaning. This could include awe in the face of nature, or hope for immortality through scientific

---

[*] Bessinger et al. (2002).
[†] Bregman (2004).

discovery. According to this view, a person could be spiritual without being religious, or religious without being spiritual.[*]

Two major approaches to definition characterize spirituality more specifically. One catalogues dimensions of religiousness/spirituality, particularly those that seem clinically relevant. For example, the Fetzer Institute/National Institute on Aging Working Group's 2003 Report *Multidimensional Measurement of Religiousness/Spirituality for Use in Health Research*[†] identified the following based on both conceptual or theoretical considerations as well as on the empirical evidence linking them to health: daily spiritual experiences, meaning, values, beliefs, forgiveness, private religious practices, religious/spiritual coping, religious support, religious/spiritual history, commitment, organizational religiousness, and religious preference. The group also considered others, such as mystical experiences, spiritual maturity and integration, hope, prayer, and compassion. A limitation of these efforts is that they result in lists of disparate categories, rather than a unifying concept.

A second major approach has been to measure spiritual well-being.[‡] For example, the Spiritual Well-Being Scale (Functional Assessment of Chronic Illness Therapy–Spiritual Well-Being

---

[*] Even individuals who do not consider themselves spiritual or religious have a philosophy of life or a world view, which Freud defined as "an intellectual construction which solves all the problems of our existence uniformly on the basis of one overriding hypothesis."

[†] Fetzer Institute (2003).

[‡] Hungelmann et al. (1996).

[FACIT-Sp]) for measuring quality of life in patients with cancer asks respondents about how much they feel a sense of purpose, peace, harmony, meaning, and so on.* However, as Koenig has pointed out, such measures of spiritual well-being reflect outcomes of spirituality, not spirituality itself.

Consider the following alternative, clinically relevant approach to characterizing the health of the soul. This approach focuses on how a relationship with the sacred, or the Other, grounds the individual's response to existential concerns such as identity, hope, meaning/purpose, morality, and autonomy/authority.

I have discussed elsewhere how the particular world view or spirituality of both patient and clinician shapes the direction of their work within each of these domains of existential concern.† By contrast, my focus here is on the nature of healthy, or helpful spirituality independent of an individual's particular world view—whether engaged or transformative versus static; integrated versus ambivalent or torn; contemplative or attuned, rather than distracted, impulsive or self-centered; mature versus developmentally delayed; feeling loved versus rejected by the Other—and on some ways of enhancing a spirituality that is healthy in each of these respects.

---

* Peterman et al. (2002).
† Peteet (2004b).

Identity

The importance of who one is within a larger context is often unmasked by life events such as a serious illness. For example, a work-oriented businessman who wonders after a heart attack if he is the same person might decide, "This experience has helped me see what I value most," or, "I know I am loved, or worthwhile because God loves me." Coming to such transcendent answers is facilitated by a spirituality that is engaged and transformative rather than static—whether in relation to the Four Noble Truths of Buddhism or the teaching of Jesus that one must lose one's life to save it.

Another term for engaged spirituality is faith. As the capacity to develop and pursue dreams, faith involves imagination, anticipation, investment, inspiration, identification, and trust, or commitment. Active faith in an experience, an ideal, a cause, or a relationship can have a powerful impact on how a person lives. Examples of individuals engaged by faith in a transforming spiritual vision include the Dalai Lama and Martin Luther King. Clinicians can foster an engaged spirituality through narrative approaches, such as Viederman and Perry's life review[*] that help patients see more clearly what their lives have been about within a bigger picture. If they have lost this sense, or if their relationship to their faith is what researchers have called "extrinsic" rather than "intrinsic," a clinician can try to help them understand why, and

---

[*] Viederman and Perry (1980).

to engage again their deepest resources of inspiration that have sustained their identity. Breitbart's meaning-centered therapy, which draws on Victor Frankl's logotherapy provides an example.[*]

Hope

When a loss or a serious illness shakes a religious person's belief in God, he or she can become cynical or despair. Patients who ground their ultimate hopes in ideals such as compassion, truth, or justice may also be vulnerable to despair if disillusioned by individuals who have represented these ideals in their lives. Whatever the objects of their faith, patients who have lost hope require a spirituality that is integrated rather than ambivalent or torn. Judith Herman points out in her book *Trauma and Recovery*[†] that a survivor of trauma needs to reconstruct a fragmented view of the world.

A hope-sustaining spirituality is one that is accessible and real to the individual not only when he is in a comforting (for example, a religious) setting, but when he is in the middle of the stress of his everyday life. The theologian Paul Tillich[‡] called this the courage to be. Many traditions encourage "spiritual disciplines" (such as prayer, worship, fasting, or giving to others) that help believers to maintain a consistent and coherent connection of their whole selves with their faith. A clinician can inquire

---

[*] Fillion et al. (2006).
[†] Herman (1997).
[‡] Tillich (1952).

about a patient's use of these as she might inquire how a patient in AA is "working the Program."

Meaning/Purpose

Many individuals bring into treatment their search for purpose and the larger meaning of their suffering.[*] An individual who loses a child to cancer may question whether his life has any purpose. A trauma survivor may question whether he can continue to believe that God is fair or loving.[†] A depressed patient who struggles with guilt may fear that he is being punished for an unpardonable sin. Whatever their world views, patients in search of meaning need a spirituality that is contemplative and attuned rather than distracted, impulsive, or self-centered. Both existentialists such as Victor Frankl[‡] and researchers such as Robert Cloninger[§] have called attention to the central role of self-transcendence in mature personality functioning.

Attunement to music, art, or nature as well as prayer and worship can all help one maintain perspective and a center of gravity outside the self. Mindfulness, acceptance, and meditation as means to this end are now taught not only by Buddhist practitioners but increasingly in psychiatric treatments such

---

[*] Yalom (1980).
[†] Peteet (2001).
[‡] Frankl (1967).
[§] Cloninger et al. (1993).

as dialectical behavioral therapy (DBT), addiction treatment programs, and to patients in general hospital settings.

Morality

Patients often present with struggles that have important moral aspects.[*] These are shaped by the individual's world view, in several ways: A person's understanding of God and of the universe shape his commitments to justice, caring, honesty, or community. Philosophical or religious ways of thinking (e.g., depending on versus questioning authority) guide the way people make moral decisions. Religious traditions both articulate standards of right and wrong and also offer options for dealing with moral failure (e.g., confession, forgiveness, making amends). Faith-based communities and community service organizations help support virtues that are basic to clinical work, such as integrity, equanimity, humility, honesty, and caring.

But regardless of differences in their world views, patients with moral concerns need a spirituality that is mature rather than developmentally delayed. Hospital chaplains often refer to the challenge of helping an adult who is facing a crisis to call upon a conception of God that goes beyond what he took from Sunday School and is more consonant with his chronological age. James Fowler[†] in his book *Stages of Faith* describes ways

---

[*] Peteet (2004a).
[†] Fowler (1981).

that faith development, like moral development, is a developmental process. A clinician might help a patient who is otherwise mature to see this and begin to "catch up," for example, by seeing the advantages of choosing mature connection and intimacy through forgiveness over the more childish satisfactions of maintaining control or of being "right."

Autonomy and Authority

The world views of religious and nonreligious individuals tend to differ most sharply on the question of their relationship to an ultimate authority. Is there an authority whom one can trust for care and direction, or does one need to rely on oneself? If God exists, is He an authority who resents His creatures' autonomy, or more like the father in Jesus' parable, more ready to receive the prodigal son home than the son imagines?

Whatever one's world view, there are benefits, as Pargament's research[*] has shown, to feeling loved rather than rejected by the Other. Clinicians can help patients to look at what kind of intimacy with God and others is possible. Is there a community that is more welcoming of the patient than he can see? Interpersonal therapeutic approaches are particularly apt here.

Any workable conception of spirituality needs to consider whether its effects are constructive, destructive, or problematic.

---

[*] Pargament (1997).

Constructive spirituality provides answers to questions of identity, hope, direction, and so forth, that help move the person toward the realization of both his own interests (such as a greater sense of peace, comfort, or joy as found in rating scales of spiritual well-being) and the interests of others. It fosters character change in mature directions and promotes more loving, harmonious relationships. For example, many individuals in Twelve Step Programs describe having moved from a life stance marked by little distance or perspective ["It's about me (and my psychology)"] and considerable projection ("Life sucks") to greater awareness ("Life is what you make of it") and a sense of satisfaction in giving back ("Can I help?").

Destructive spirituality fosters narrow devotion to causes or objects of worship that damage others when they do not worship the same parochial gods. Examples would include religiously sanctioned racism or persecution, and suicide bombing.

Problematic spirituality challenges the status quo, in the tradition of prophets who "speak the truth to power." Whether one considers this kind of spirituality constructive or destructive depends to a large degree on one's view of the nature of the ultimate Other and of what is best for human beings. For example: Is compassion important enough to justify the self-immolation of Buddhist monks during the war in Vietnam? Does God value sacrifice to the point of martyrdom? Sacrifice to the point of suffering? How does one balance the claims of this life versus those of the next, or balance those of self-interest and obligations to others? Depressed patients sometimes ask clinicians for help in struggling with these questions.

Potential Objections

There are a number of potential obstacles to acceptance by mental health professionals of the view presented here that the health of the heart, mind, and soul are clinically important, intimately related, and yet distinct. One of the oldest is dualistic, traceable to Plato's distinction between body and mind, and to the later contributions of Descartes. Cartesian dualism, as Kendler[*] and Miresco and Kirmayer[†] remind us, remains an active assumptive stance within psychiatry, serving to impede integrative thought and research. The correlate of dualism—reductionism—continues to operate when clinicians approach complex relationships among thoughts, emotions, values, and spiritual experiences in simplistic, single-paradigm ways. For example: Freud famously attempted to reduce spirituality to wish-fulfillment. Biologically oriented psychiatrists sometimes attempt to explain spiritual experience and depression solely in terms of the findings of neuroimaging or of measures of serotonin activity. The prominence in our culture's thinking of pharmaceutical approaches to depressive conditions is well known.[‡] As we will see in subsequent chapters, conservative religious believers sometimes

---

[*] Kendler (2005).
[†] Miresco and Kirmayer (2006).
[‡] Horwitz and Wakefield (2007).

embrace another problematic form of reductionism that attempts to explain emotional or mental problems in spiritual terms. The approach adopted here is consistent with Kendler's[*] "explanatory pluralism," which suggests the need to identify divergent levels of analysis before attempting to incorporate them into a larger picture.

A more subtle challenge comes from postmodernism, according to which the impossibility of a purely objective point of reference invalidates the question of what is true.[†] Taking a postmodern stance can encourage clinicians to regard questions of value, commitment, and faith as unanswerable and therefore unimportant. The results may be to discount the life of the soul, to truncate their view of health, and to collude with the disillusionment of their patients. But a clinician need not believe in God to recognize the importance of a search for truth and ideals by which to live and die.

A third objection is that to link the terms health and spirituality is to participate in the "tyranny of health," or the moralistic overmedicalization of problems in living. A number of critics[‡,§,¶] have called attention to American society's propensity to turn human problems including character flaws, unattractiveness,

---

[*] Kendler (2005).

[†] McGowan (1991).

[‡] Illich (1974).

[§] Barsky (1988).

[¶] Fitzgerald (1994).

poverty, and violence into objects of therapeutic intervention. They point out that too often the results have been to encourage individuals to expect that they can escape unhappiness, pain, stress, or death. Envisioning health to include spiritual health does run this risk if it endorses pursuing spirituality for its health benefits. Shuman and Meador have recently addressed this directly in their recent book *Heal Thyself: Spirituality, Medicine and the Distortion of Christianity*[*] Sloan et al.[†] go further to criticize spiritual care by clinicians on similar grounds, arguing that medical and spiritual domains should remain conceptually and clinically separate.

But my contention is that optimal human functioning includes a relationship with the transcendent which clinicians need to take into account in treating the whole person. This relationship need not add to the tyranny of health, so long as health does not become an object of worship or an excuse for moralism. Rather, the necessity for debate about what the goals of health care should be makes clear the importance of taking a larger frame of reference into account.

In summary, we began with the premise that clinicians need a concept of healthy human functioning in order to clearly define the goals of treatment. We then saw, consistent with both neurobiology and the major therapeutic schools, that optimal or

---

[*] Shuman and Meador (2003).
[†] Sloan et al. (2000).

healthy human functioning involves the integration of emotion, volition, coping, cognition, and a relationship to reality that transcends the self. After noting the limitations of two prevalent ways of describing this transcendent relationship, we suggested that a clinician can more usefully regard spirituality as the individual's response to existential concerns in areas such as identity, hope, meaning/purpose, morality, and autonomy/ultimate authority. Finally, we considered negative spirituality, pitfalls encountered in attempting to incorporate spirituality into clinical practice, and potential objections to doing so. The chapters that follow consider the implications of this view for understanding the relationship between depression and spirituality, and how clinicians can help depressed patients work not only toward relief of painful symptoms, but toward full health.

References

Ainslie, G. (2005). Precis of breakdown of will. *Behav Brain Sci,* 28, 635–650; discussion 650–673.

American Psychiatric Association (1994). *Diagnostic and Statistical Manual of Mental Disorders.* Washington, DC: American Psychiatric Publishing, Inc.

American Psychiatric Association. (2005). Use of the Concept of Recovery. http://www.psych.org/edu/other_res/lib_archives/archives/200504.pdf; accessed March 11, 2007.

Barsky, A.J. (1988). The paradox of health. *N Engl J Med,* 318, 414–418.

Ben-Arye, E., Bar-Sela, G., Frenkel, M., Kuten, A., & Hermoni, D. (2006). Is a biopsychosocial-spiritual approach relevant to cancer treatment? A study of patients and oncology staff members on issues of complementary medicine and spirituality. *Support Care Cancer,* 14, 147–152.

Bessinger, D., & Kuhne, T. (2002). Medical spirituality: Defining domains and boundaries. *South Med J,* 95, 1385–1388.

Bregman, L. (2004). Defining spirituality: Multiple uses and murky meanings of an incredibly popular term. *J Pastoral Care Counsel,* 58, 157–167.

Carr, A. (2004). *Positive Psychology: The Science of Happiness and Human Strengths.* New York: Brunner-Routledge.

Cloninger, C.R., Svrakic, D.M., & Przybeck, T.R. (1993). A psychobiological model of temperament and character. *Arch Gen Psychiatry,* 50, 975–990.

Curlin, F.A., Lantos, J.D., Roach, C.J., Sellergren, S.A., & Chin, M.H. (2005). Religious characteristics of U.S. physicians: A national survey. *J Gen Intern Med,* 20, 629–634.

Engel, G.L. (1978). The biopsychosocial model and the education of health professionals. *Ann N Y Acad Sci,* 310, 169–187.

Farber, L.H. (1966). *The Ways of the Will: Essays Toward a Psychology and Psychopathology of Will.* New York: Basic Books.

Fetzer Institute. (2003). Multidimensional measurement of religiousness/spirituality for use in health research: A report of the Fetzer Institute/National Institute of Aging Working Group. Kalamazoo, MI: Fetzer Institute.

Fillion, L., Dupuis, R., Tremblay, I., De Grace, G.R., & Breitbart, W. (2006). Enhancing meaning in palliative care practice: A meaning-centered intervention to promote job satisfaction. *Palliat Support Care,* 4, 333–344.

Fitzgerald, F.T. (1994). The tyranny of health. *N Engl J Med,* 331, 196–198.

Fowler, J.W. (1981). *Stages of Faith: The Psychology of Human Development and the Quest for Meaning* (1st ed.). San Francisco: Harper & Row.

Frankl, V.E., & Crumbaugh, J.C. (1967). *Psychotherapy and Existentialism: Selected Papers on Logotherapy.* New York: Simon and Schuster.

Fredrickson, B.L. (2001). The role of positive emotions in positive psychology. The broaden-and-build theory of positive emotions. *Am Psychol,* 66, 218–226.

Fredrickson, B.L., & Losada, M.F. (2005). Positive affect and the complex dynamics of human flourishing. *Am Psychol,* 60, 678–686.

Freud, S. (1923). *The Ego and the Id.* New York: W.W. Norton and Company.

Havens, L.L. (1973). *Approaches to the Mind: Movement of the Psychiatric Schools From Sects Toward Science* (1st ed.). Boston: Little Brown.

Havens, L.L. (1984). The need for tests of normal functioning in the psychiatric interview. *Am J Psychiatry,* 141(10), 1208–1211.

Hayes, S.C., Strosahl, K.D., & Wilson, K.G. (1999). *Acceptance and Commitment Therapy: An Experimental Approach to Behavior Change.* New York: Guilford.

Herman, J.L. (1997). *Trauma and Recovery* (Rev. ed.). New York: Basic Books.

Horwitz, A.V., & Wakefield, J.C. (2007). *The Loss of Sadness: How Psychiatry Transformed Normal Sorrow Into Depressive Disorder.* New York: Oxford University Press.

Hungelmann, J., Kenkel-Rossi, E., Klassen, L., & Stollenwerk, R. (1996). Focus on spiritual well-being: Harmonious interconnectedness of mind-body-spirit—Use of the JAREL spiritual well-being scale. *Geriatr Nurs,* 17, 262–266.

Illich, I. (1974). Medical nemesis. *Lancet,* 1, 918–921.

Kendler, K.S. (2005). Toward a philosophical structure for psychiatry. *Am J Psychiatry,* 162, 433–440.

Lazare, A. (1973). Hidden conceptual models in clinical psychiatry. *N Engl J Med,* 288, 345–351.

Liberman, R.P., & Kopelowicz, A. (2005). Recovery from schizophrenia: A concept in search of research. *Psychiatr Serv,* 56, 735–742.

Lukoff, D. (2007). Spirituality in the recovery from persistent mental disorders. *South Med J,* 100, 642–646.

May, R. (1969). *Love and Will* (1st ed.). New York: Norton.

McGowan, J. (1991). *Postmodernism and Its Critics.* Ithaca, NY: Cornell University Press.

McHugh, P.R., & Slavney, P.R. (1998). *The Perspectives of Psychiatry* (2nd ed.). Baltimore: Johns Hopkins University Press.

Miresco, M.J., & Kirmayer, L.J. (2006). The persistence of mind-brain dualism in psychiatric reasoning about clinical scenarios. *Am J Psychiatry,* 163, 913–919.

Pargament, K.I. (1997). *The Psychology of Religion and Coping: Theory, Research, Practice.* New York: Guilford Press.

Peteet, J.R. (2001). Putting suffering into perspective: Implications of the patient's world view. *J Psychother Pract Res,* 10, 187–192.

Peteet, J.R. (2004a). *Doing the Right Thing: An Approach to Moral Issues in Mental Health Treatment.* Washington, DC: American Psychiatric Publishing, Inc.

Peteet, J.R. (2004b). Therapeutic implications of world view. In A.M. Josephson & J.R. Peteet (Eds.), *Handbook of Spirituality and World View in Clinical Practice.* Washington, DC: American Psychiatric Publishing, Inc.

Peterman, A.H., Fitchett, G., Brady, M.J., Hernandez, L., & Cella, D. (2002). Measuring spiritual well-being in people with cancer: The functional assessment of chronic illness therapy—Spiritual Well-being Scale (FACIT-Sp). *Ann Behav Med,* 24, 49–58.

Schafer, R. (2003). *Bad Feelings: Selected Psychoanalytic Essays.* New York: Other Press.

Seligman, M.E., Steen, T.A., Park, N., & Peterson, C. (2005). Positive psychology progress: Empirical validation of interventions. *Am Psychol,* 60, 410–421.

Shuman, J.J., & Meador, K.G. (2003). *Heal Thyself: Spirituality, Medicine, and the Distortion of Christianity.* New York: Oxford University Press.

Siegel, D. (2007). *The Mindful Brain: Reflection and Attunement in the Cultivation of Well-Being.* New York: Norton Press.

Sloan, R.P., Bagiella, E., VandeCreek, L., Hover, M., Casalone, C., Jinpu Hirsch, T., et al. (2000). Should physicians prescribe religious activities? *N Engl J Med,* 242, 1913–1916.

Sulmasy, D.P. (2002). A biopsychosocial-spiritual model for the care of patients at the end of life. *Gerontologist,* 42 Spec No 3, 24–33.

Tillich, P. (1952). *The Courage to Be.* New Haven, CT: Yale University Press.

Vaillant, G.E. (2003). Mental health. *Am J Psychiatry,* 160(8), 1373–1384.

Vaillant, G.E., & Harvard University. Dept. of Hygiene. (1977). *Adaptation to Life* (1st ed.). Boston: Little, Brown.

Verhagen, P. Personal communication. September 29, 2008.

Viederman, M., & Perry, S.W., 3rd. (1980). Use of a psychodynamic life narrative in the treatment of depression in the physically ill. *Gen Hosp Psychiatry,* 2, 177–185.

Weissman, M.M., Markowitz, J.C., & Klerman, G.L. (2000). *Comprehensive Guide to Interpersonal Psychotherapy.* New York: Basic Books.

Yalom, I.D. (1980). *Existential Psychotherapy.* New York: Basic Books.

2 Depression and Spirituality

But ah, but O thou terrible, why wouldst thou rude on me
Thy wring-world right foot rock? Lay a lionlimb against me? scan
With darksome devouring eyes my bruised bones? and fan,
O in turns of tempest, me heaped there; me frantic to avoid thee
   and flee?

Carrion Comfort, Gerard Manley Hopkins

For Hopkins, as for many others, depression and spiritual experience are intertwined. Questions that believers ask in attempting to disentangle them include: Is my despondency an illness, a way of responding to adversity, or an indication that something is wrong in my life? Is my despair a failure of spiritual will, a trial of my faith, or a punishment? In this chapter I explore the relationship between depression and the spiritual self. Specifically, I (1) consider the existential struggles of depressed individuals, and their search for spiritual answers; (2) review current empirical literature on depression and spirituality; (3) compare the perspectives of various spiritual traditions or world views; and (4) summarize ways that spirituality and depression interact. These considerations will ground inclusion in the next chapter of spirituality in the differential diagnosis and clinical formulation of depressive states.

Existential Struggles

Depression undermines a person's response to the conditions of existence—his sense of who he is, what he can hope for, what meaning his life has, and whether or not he is alone and cared for. In turn, harsh conditions of existence such as a lack of security or rest, as well as the struggles of individuals to understand the meaning of loss or adversity, can contribute to depression. Consider some of the ways that depressed patients search for answers to existential questions and experience spiritual distress until they find them.

IDENTITY

Serious depression can separate individuals from interests, goals, and relationships that have previously helped to define them. As Karp[*] puts it, "Depression steals away whoever you were, prevents you from seeing who you might someday be, and replaces your life with a black hole."

Conversely, loss of a valued job, role, or relationship may raise troubling doubts about who one is. A person experiencing financial ruin might ask himself, "Am I worthwhile even if I am

---
[*] Karp (1996, p. 24).

no longer able to provide for my family?" Or a person who experiences depression after a failed relationship might wonder, "Am I someone who is so unrealistic or insatiable that I am doomed to unhappiness?"

> A graduate student in her twenties came for help with depression after breaking up with a boyfriend. She could see that he had neglected her needs and was likely to continue doing so, but ruminated about whether she was unlovable and a failure at relationships. As the most "sensitive" of her siblings, she had also wondered if she was responsible for her father's frequent absences during business trips. When depressed, she found medication and insight somewhat helpful, but attributed her improvement to feeling loved by God.

Similar to the way in which alcoholics can find a new identity in a Twelve Step Program,[*] individuals shaken by a life crisis sometimes undergo conversion to a new religious identity.[†]

Hope

The hopelessness that is a hallmark of serious depression, which often entails pessimism,[‡] has a spiritual dimension. "Depression is for many people an experience of being cast out by God or abandoned by Him, and many who have been depressed say they are unable to believe in a God who inflicts such cruelty so

---

[*] Peteet (1993).

[†] Rambo (1993).

[‡] Beck et al. (1985).

uselessly on the members of his flock."* Depressive hopelessness can reflect a failure of basic trust with roots in betrayal by other authorities who did not act to prevent abuse or neglect.

> A 50-year-old divorced secretary began treatment for chronic depression with suicidal ideation. After growing up in a physically and verbally abusive home, she "escaped" by marrying a controlling man who became increasingly paranoid and violent. Following a divorce she became isolated and depressed. Psychotherapy and a day hospital program helped her to deal with her losses. However, recalling details of her childhood trauma made her feel permanently damaged, particularly when she recognized in herself a pattern of looking for others to rescue her, and then of withdrawing or attacking when they disappointed her. In a parallel process of withdrawing in disappointment, she experienced God as uncaring for allowing such damage, withdrew, and experienced this as a further loss.

Solomon[†] highlights the dynamic way that depression can complicate the process of rebuilding one's world view following trauma[‡]:

> You survive depression through a faith in life that is as abstract as any religious belief system. Depression is the most cynical thing in the world, but it is also the origin of a kind of belief. To endure it and emerge as yourself is to find that what you did not have the courage to hope may yet prove true. The discourse of faith, like that of romantic love, has the disadvantage that it carries the potential for disillusionment. (p. 130)

---

[*] Solomon (2001).
[†] Solomon (2001).
[‡] Herman (1997).

Meaning / Purpose

Depression is well known for sapping life of its meaning and purpose. But clinicians are also familiar with the way that the loss of a source of meaning in one's life can precipitate depression.

> A 65-year-old previously active engineer diagnosed with multiple myeloma became acutely despondent after becoming incapacitated by back pain. He attempted suicide by taking an overdose of pills, explaining later that he could not imagine leading an unproductive life.

Similarly, individuals who pursue pleasure or power can become depressed when the limitations of these goals become clear.

But does a loss of culturally shared meaning also contribute to depression? French existentialists and playwrights famously linked the darkness of a world devoid of meaning to personal despair in works such as Sartre's *No Exit* and *Nausea*. Camus put it starkly in *The Myth of Sisyphus*: "There is but one truly serious philosophical problem, and that is suicide."

Many observers have linked increasing rates of depression to disruptive societal factors that contribute to loss of personal meaning: Emil Durkheim in his famous study of suicide[*] correlated rates of suicide with social integration. Alvin Toffler in *Future Shock*[†] documented the disorienting features of rapid

---

[*] Durkheim (1951).
[†] Toffler (1970).

social change. In his seminal book *Rethinking Psychiatry: From Cultural Category to Personal Experience,* Arthur Kleinman[*] presented compelling cross-cultural evidence that depression is more than simply the result of biology. Todd Gitlin, in *Media Unlimited: How the Torrent of Images and Sounds Overwhelms Our Lives,*[†] argued that the pressure of chaotic messages in our society leads to depressive withdrawal and isolation. Edward Hallowell, in his book *Crazy Busy,*[‡] highlighted the appeal of our culture's busyness: "At the deepest level—the level we rarely visit—we stay busy to *avoid* looking into the abyss" (p. 11). David Karp, in *Speaking of Sadness: Depression, Disconnection, and the Meanings of Illness,*[§] tied postmodern disillusionment directly to contemporary experiences of depression. Dan Blazer, in *The Age of Melancholy: "Major Depression" and Its Social Origins,*[¶] called for greater attention to patients' cultural context and world views. And Cardinal Barrigan,[**] representing the Vatican at a council of health care workers, encouraged them to see increasing rates of depression as understandable since postmodern culture is "empty of values, founded on well-being and pleasure, in which economic profit counts as the supreme goal."

---

[*] Kleinman (1988).
[†] Gitlin (2001).
[‡] Hallowell (2007).
[§] Karp (1996, pp. 165–187).
[¶] Blazer (2005).
[**] Conroy (2004).

Morality

John Donne conveyed in his "Holy Sonnet III" the circularity of guilt in depression[*]:

> To (poore) me is allow'd
> No ease; for, long, yet vehement griefe hath beene
> Th'effect and cause, the punishment and sinne.

For the depressed individual, forgiveness can seem inaccessible, if not incomprehensible. Self-loathing, writes William Styron,[†] is depression's "premier badge."

Distress over moral failure is common in patients coming for outpatient treatment.[‡] Inability to resolve guilt, for example over neglect or abuse of one's children, can also be an important contributor to depression. Once he is depressed, a patient's guilt can then become irrational, magnified, even overwhelming.

> A 50-year-old Protestant married father of three presented for treatment preoccupied with feeling "evil." He had been without significant psychiatric symptoms until several years previously when his parents, in their eighties, moved near him with expectations that he would help care for them. Instead, he developed incapacitating fatigue and difficulty concentrating. After failed trials of antidepressant medication, he accepted disability for chronic fatigue syndrome. Financial considerations forced the family to move to another state, where he ruminated about having sold their home under false pretenses, and about fraudulently collecting disability.

---

[*] Hopkins (1918).
[†] Styron (1990).
[‡] Kroll et al. (2004).

History revealed that he had never been able to confront his critical father, who had blamed the children for their mother's tuberculosis. On examination the patient was thin, restless, reporting poor sleep, inability to enjoy anything, doubts about "everything I thought I believed in," and guilt for being unable to function as a father and husband. Family members and a pastor tried without success to reason with him about his sense of guilt. Eventually, he responded to their encouragement to allow time for medication, an activity program, and psychotherapy to have their effects.

This patient's failure to either confront or comply with his moralistic father's new demands led to emotional incapacitation, then to an agitated depression with a psychotic level of guilt over his emotional paralysis.

Autonomy / Authority

Depressed individuals tend to withdraw from important sources of support because they feel unloved or judged by others, or burdensome to them. Spiritual and/or religious individuals who become depressed may feel not only distant from God but punished and judged by Him. Pargament[*] has referred to this as negative religious coping.

A mother in her thirties began to contemplate suicide after learning that chemotherapy was no longer controlling the growth of her 10-year-old son's brain tumor. Her husband, a truck driver, helped out with their son but seemed unable to share his own feelings or to tolerate her grief. As a child, she had coped with physical and verbal

---

[*] Pargament (1997).

abuse from her alcoholic parents by "putting up a wall" and by fighting for what she needed. She had softened this cynical stance only after her son had brightened her life. Suicide appealed to her as a way of joining him after he died, but she feared that God would "frown on this" and punish her. She had turned to the God she had first imagined in parochial school when her son became ill, but He seemed to become menacing and confusing as her son's illness progressed. She wondered how she could expect anything good in life from Him after He failed to save her son. Was He as untrustworthy as other authorities in her life had been?

Nonreligious individuals who become depressed may also feel more alone in the universe. Isolation and estrangement can be important factors in either initiating or maintaining depression. As such, they are the primary targets of interpersonal psychotherapy for depression.[*]

In summary, patients' real and magnified concerns in areas such as identity, hope, meaning/purpose, morality, and autonomy/authority are often central to their experience of depression. We consider the treatment implications of these concerns in Chapter 4.

Research

Well over 100 studies have explored the relationship between depression and religiousness or spirituality. Koenig et al.,[†] Smith

---

[*] Weissman et al. (2007).

[†] Koenig et al. (2001).

et al.,[*] and Koenig[†] concluded from their reviews that despite methodological inconsistencies the majority of these show less depression among the more religious. They note a buffering effect of religion on depressive symptoms, or improved recovery in populations stressed by chronic physical disability, sexual assault, loss of or caring for an ill relative, natural disasters, and economic hardship. In 15 of the 22 of longitudinal studies considered, greater religiousness at baseline predicted lower depression scores at follow up.

McCullough and Larsen's[‡] meta-analysis of eight clinical trials of religious interventions found a positive effect on depression of religious interventions conducted using Muslim, Christian, and Buddhist perspectives. Some investigators incorporated religious content into secular forms of psychotherapy. For example, in a randomized study of religious cognitive behavioral therapy (CBT), Probst et al.[§] compared the efficacy of standard and religiously based CBT, delivered by both religious and nonreligious therapists, and a pastoral counseling intervention delivered by religious therapists in a population of 59 depressed Christian outpatients who had been ill for an average of a year. Religiously based CBT was more effective than standard CBT, whether delivered by a religious or a nonreligious therapist.

---

[*] Smith et al. (2003).
[†] Koenig (2005).
[‡] McCullough and Larson (1999).
[§] Probst et al. (1992).

Azhar and Varma[*] used a randomized clinical trial to compare the effects of the addition of 45-minute weekly psychotherapy that involved reading verses from the Holy Qur'an and saying Muslim prayers to standard psychotherapy and medication alone in a group of 64 Malaysians with strong Muslim backgrounds. The investigators found faster recovery as measured by raters blind to the treatment in the additional intervention group.

What could be the mechanism of this generally positive association between religion and outcome in depression? Studies of religious involvement distinguishing public from private activity have generally, though not consistently, shown more effect of organized activity.[†,‡] On the other hand, extrinsic measures of religiosity have sometimes correlated more with depression than measures of intrinsic religious motivation. Studies such as that of Koenig et al.[§] of religious belief and coping with medical illness have found a more benevolent appraisal of God to be less associated with depression than one of God as punishing or unable to affect their situation. More longitudinal data supports this finding than the effects of public activity and intrinsic motivation. A summary conclusion would be that available cross-sectional research suggests that both organizational and nonorganizational religious

---

[*] Azhar and Varma (1995).
[†] Koenig et al. (2001).
[‡] Maselko et al. (2008).
[§] Koenig et al. (1998).

activity is associated with a significantly lower likelihood of depression at points of stress. More work is needed to clarify the role of religion in coping and vulnerability to depression.

Studies increasingly distinguish spirituality from religiosity, and measures of spiritual well-being have proliferated. These include the Functional Assessment of Chronic Illness Therapy (FACIT) Spiritual Well Being Scale,[*] the Spirituality Index of Well-Being Scale,[†] the Spiritual Well-Being Scale (SWBS),[‡] and the Spiritual Transcendence Scale.[§] Nelson et al.[¶] found in a study of 162 individuals with a life expectancy of less than 6 months that high scores of spiritual well-being (in particular the meaning and peace subscales of the FACIT) but not measures of religiosity correlated with lower scores on the Hamilton Depression Rating Scale. Coleman and Holzemer[**] similarly reported that, in a sample of 117 African American men living with HIV disease, existential well-being as indicated by meaning and purpose correlated more closely than religious well-being with participants' psychological well-being. McCoubrie and Davies[††] also reported effects of spiritual but not religious well-being on depression in a sample of patients with advanced

---

[*] Peterman et al. (2002).
[†] Daaleman et al. (2002).
[‡] Bufford et al. (1991).
[§] Piedmont (1999).
[¶] Nelson et al. (2002).
[**] Coleman and Holzemer (1999).
[††] McCoubrie and Davies (2006).

cancer. On the other hand, Wink et al.[*] found in a longitudinal community-based study that religiousness, but not spirituality defined as use of noninstitutionalized religious beliefs and practices, showed a buffering effect on depression associated with poor physical health. Similarly, Maselko and colleagues[†] study of the lifetime risk of major depression in the New England Family Cohort (N = 918), revealed a lower risk of depression in subjects with higher attendance at religious services and higher scores of existential well-being, but a 1.5 fold increase in risk in those reporting a closer relationship with a higher power (suggesting to the authors that prayer may be used to cope with depression, and that involvement with others in a faith-based community may be protective).

Other investigators have found measures of spirituality inversely correlated with depressive symptoms in the elderly,[‡,§] survivors of domestic violence,[¶] palliative care inpatients,[**] primary care outpatients,[††] and patients with rheumatoid arthritis,[‡‡]

---

[*] Wink et al. (2005).
[†] Maselko et al. (2008).
[‡] Springer et al. (2003).
[§] Fry (2000).
[¶] Gillum et al. (2006).
[**] McClain et al. (2003).
[††] Daaleman et al. (2006).
[‡‡] Bartlett et al. (2003).

HIV disease,[*] and cancer.[†] Boscaglia et al.[‡] found spirituality predictive of positive affect in patients with rheumatoid arthritis.

Kaye and colleagues'[§] literature review offers several possibilities by which the effects of spirituality on depression could be mediated, including by increasing a sense of control, by helping individuals reframe stressful events, through the use of imagery, and/or via neuroendocrine pathways. Others have asked whether the beneficial effects of spirituality might be mediated by forgiveness.[¶] Unfortunately, measures of spirituality used in research to date remain less consistent and coherent than those used to study religiosity. Self-transcendence, connection, and meaning are common themes, but the inclusion within these instruments of indices of well-being, or peace, which are positive *outcomes* of spirituality, makes correlations that have been found with positive emotions somewhat tautological and difficult to interpret.

In any case, sizable groups of patients want spirituality included in their care when depressed. In a national Internet-based survey Givens et al.[**] found that ethnic minorities other than Native Americans preferred counseling and prayer to medication for depression (more than twice as often as whites). Similarly, in an exploratory study of factors important to depression care in

---

[*] Carrico et al. (2006).
[†] Krupski et al. (2006).
[‡] Boscaglia et al. (2005).
[§] Kaye and Raghavan (2002).
[¶] Levenson et al. (2006).
[**] Givens et al. (2007).

76 clinic patients with minor depression, Cooper et al.[*] found that compared with whites, African American patients gave higher ratings to all items related to spirituality. These aspects of care, which included having faith in God, being able to ask God for forgiveness, and prayer were among the 10 most important aspects of depression care for African Americans. Cunningham et al.[†] found in a sample of 18 Dublin adults interviewed about their depression that 64 percent reported using one or more of the following religious coping strategies: praying for guidance and strength, seeing God's help, or trying to find "comfort in my religion." Those who did not use such strategies showed higher scores of depressive severity. These findings highlight the clinical importance of appreciating a patient's cultural and religious understanding of depression, as well as the spiritual practices or beliefs that might help them.

Traditions

What difference does the patient's world view make in understanding and approaching his depression?

JEWS

Unlike classical Greeks, whose gods were rarely interested in humans, and who regarded suicide as a noble way of escape

---

[*] Cooper et al. (2001).
[†] Cunningham et al. (2007).

through asserting one's freedom, Jews believe that God cares for his children.* When Job suffers he is never abandoned. When psalmists feel overwhelmed, question whether they should go on, and cry out to God they find that he is there to engage them, though (as in Job's case) not always in the ways they expect. Psalm 69 is one of several that express despair to God:

> Save me, O God, for the waters have come up to my neck.
> I sink in the miry depths, where there is no foothold. I have come into the deep waters; the floods engulf me.
> I am worn out calling for help; my throat is parched. My eyes fail, looking for my God.

When Elijah hides in the desert in fear of Jezebel and asks to be allowed to die, God does not scold, but comforts and feeds him before revealing himself. Other scriptures recognize the irrational power of depression, as seen in the dark moods of King Saul that were soothed by music.

Rabbinic teaching distinguishes two types of human failures to serve God with joy. The person who is listless, tends to withdraw into sleep, dislikes himself or others, and is filled with anger is sad because of an arrogant expectation that he is entitled to more in the spiritual as well as the material realm. A healthier kind of sorrow, "tinged with bitterness rather than self-pity," leads to renewed study or prayer.†

---

* Kaplan and Schwartz (2000).
† Yisra\U+02be\eli (1760/1981).

God's forgiveness is central in dealing with human failure and guilt, as evident in the annual celebration of Yom Kippur, which includes the ritual communal recitation of prayer, confession of sin, and request for forgiveness.

CHRISTIANS

Like Jews, Christians believe that they belong to God, and that they find their highest joy in an intimate relationship with Him—the term *joy* appears 65 times in the New Testament scriptures.

Jesus reached out with compassion to heal people who suffered mental as well as physical disorders, restoring them to being "calm" and in their "right mind." The early church saw the failures of believers as reasons to pray and, where needed, find forgiveness.

Jesus' early followers also believed they would suffer as he did for doing what was right. Giving thanks in, or even for, adversity kept them aware of their need for God and helped to build needed character:

> More than that, we rejoice in our sufferings, knowing that suffering produces endurance, and endurance produces character, and character produces hope, and hope does not disappoint us because the love of God has been poured into our hearts… (Romans 5:3–5)

Mystics such as St. John of the Cross described benefits of suffering through periods of doubt and inability to sense God's presence, which he called the *Dark Night of the Soul*.* At the same

---
* John of the Cross (1990).

time, New Testament writers such as Paul cautioned against becoming weary in the pursuit of the good. John Bunyan in *Pilgrim's Progress* similarly warned against falling into the Slough of Despond.

Christians over the centuries have applied scripture in very different ways with regard to depression. William James's classic distinction in *The Varieties of Religious Experience: A Study in Human Nature*[*] between the "once-" and "twice-born" may contain a partial explanation. The "twice-born," who see facing one's failure as a requirement for change, appeal to an individual's sense of guilt and need for dramatic help from God. Because the "twice-born" are less interested in psychological or biological explanations, their prescriptions for depression can seem to mental health professionals unbalanced, otherworldly, and/or judgmental. Examples include Tim LaHaye's *How to Win Over Depression*[†] and Jay Adams' *Competent to Counsel*.[‡]

The "once-born," found more often in mainstream Protestant denominations, see emotional and spiritual growth as related processes that require time. As a result, they focus on enlisting biological, psychological, and spiritual resources in the service of healing. Examples include pastoral psychotherapy aimed at the encouragement of positive religious coping, and the use of forgiveness in psychotherapy. Despite, or perhaps because of their

---

[*] James (1902).
[†] LaHaye (1974).
[‡] Adams (1972).

growing popularity, these approaches have raised a number of concerns: Blazer[*] sees little actual difference between the practice of pastoral and secular counselors. Jones[†] points out that an emphasis on religious coping, which can be helpful, does not address the core interest of religion in transformation. Shuman and Meador[‡] charge that promoting faith-based therapies because they improve health distorts Christianity, since health is not its highest value.

In his 1998 book *Freud Versus God: How Psychiatry Lost Its Soul and Christianity Lost Its Mind*,[§] Blazer called for discussion of ways to transcend the divide between psychological and spiritual approaches to problems such as depression. The decade since has seen a growing emphasis on spiritual practices or disciplines as a path to integration. Minister and psychoanalyst James Jones[¶] frames the solution this way:

> ... having a good theory about God will not lead to further spiritual development unless that theory is also a guide to practice, to doing something new or doing something familiar in a new way. So again, in the spiritual journey, theory should give rise to practice—in this case, perhaps, meditation, prayer, liturgical participation, feeding the hungry, visiting the sick, reaching out to the distraught. And practice should generate new experiences—a deeper realization of the presence of God, a new awareness of places of alienation and falling

---

[*] Blazer (1998, p. 83).

[†] Jones (2003, p. 161).

[‡] Shuman and Meador (2003).

[§] Blazer (1998).

[¶] Jones (2003).

short and their cure, new vistas of peace and tranquility, a greater experience of the religious community. These new experiences, and others like them, are the heart of transformation. (p. 162)

Other Christian descriptions of the healing potential of this kind of active, emotional engagement in spiritual practices are Richard Foster's *Celebration of Discipline: The Path to Spiritual Growth*,[*] Dallas Willard's *The Spirit of the Disciplines: Understanding How God Changes Lives*,[†] and Gerald May's *The Dark Night of the Soul: A Psychiatrist Explores the Connection Between Darkness and Spiritual Growth*.[‡] While aiming primarily toward spiritual healing, these authors regard both emotional and cognitive participation in this process as central to the transformation of the whole person that results from an enhanced relationship with God. Protestants as well as Catholics have become increasingly interested in spiritual direction, and in small groups focused on prayer for emotional as well as other concerns. Churches such as the Vineyard Christian Fellowship that integrate healing, feeling, and traditional faith have grown dramatically.[§] A depressed person in such a church might ask others for prayer for healing, explore emotional concerns related to his spiritual life in his small group, engage in a formal program such as Living Waters for addressing "relational brokenness" (that

---

[*] Foster (1978).
[†] Willard (1998).
[‡] May (2004).
[§] Jackson, (1999).

is, trauma or character-based vulnerabilities to depression), and accept a referral for therapy or medication.

The Roman Catholic Church has at times seen depression as both potentially spiritual in origin and deserving of special help. For example, Pope John Paul II told participants at the November 2003 XVIII International Conference of the Pontifical Council for Health Care Workers that depression could often be a spiritual trial, and that those suffering deserve support from their priests and parish communities.[*] The Ignatian Exercises (consisting of stages of confession, explanation, expiation, and transformation, each accompanied by visualization, prayer, and reflection) are for Jesuit Catholics an important means of psychological and spiritual integration.[†,‡]

Buddhists

The Four Noble Truths form the basic framework of the Buddhist understanding of suffering and self-healing. They hold that the human condition is governed by tendencies to misknowledge (*avidya*) or self-involvement (*amagraha*) and unhealthy (*akusala-samskara*) or addictive emotion (*klia-samskara*). These contribute to an unhealthy cycle of stereotyped, reactive, and compulsive experience and behavior. Freedom from reacting in these ways comes through following

---

[*] Conroy (2004).

[†] Meadow (1989).

[‡] Meissner (1999).

eight steps that can be simplified as the disciplines of wisdom (*prajna*), meditation (*samadhi*), and ethics (*sila*). Put more simply, Buddhists teach that selfishness causes most depression, and that compassion (including for oneself), loving kindness, and mindfulness are important in overcoming the self-absorption that is at its core. To quote the Buddha: "We are shaped by our thoughts; we become what we think. When the mind is pure, joy follows like a shadow that never leaves."[*] Many Buddhists would also acknowledge that more serious forms of depression such as major depression and bipolar disorder require professional treatment. But they would affirm what cognitive behavioral therapists recognize as a core skill in freeing oneself from depression: "to recognize and disengage from mind states characterized by self-perpetuating patterns of ruminative, negative thought."[†] Reminiscent of Jones's comment about transformation in the Christian tradition, Segal et al. explain the working model of mindfulness in treating depression this way:

> At the heart of this state of mind is a particular 'view' or 'model' of depressive experience. Within this view, the self is seen (or more precisely, felt) as inadequate, worthless and blameworthy, and negative thoughts are seen as accurate reflections of reality. This view, or model, is much more than simply a collection of concepts or ideas about the self and depression. Rather, it represents the distilled essence of many experiences of mind, feelings, and body. This essence is represented at a deeper level than the purely conceptual. If

---

[*] A View on Buddhism: Depression (2004).
[†] Segal et al. (2002, p. 75).

we are to make changes at this deeper level, we need to do more than provide patients with new conceptual information about depression, negative thinking, and relapse. Instead, we need to provide new experiences for the mind and body, over and over again, that will accumulate to create an alternative view (p. 67).

Hindus

Hindus also understand the mind as the source of both bondage and liberation. The Ayurvedic tradition emphasizes balance among the three elements of wind, water, and fire that govern movement, cohesiveness, and metabolism, respectively. Hindus are apt to see distress as due to an imbalance among these humors, and depression as contextual—related to an imbalance among the body, the spirit, and the environment. However, unlike Westerners who emphasize grieving, Hindus traditionally regard feelings of depression among victims of loss as unhealthy and negative. Their preferred solution is to pursue inner peace[*] and sattva (knowledge and purity), through one of four spiritual paths that best fits the individual: knowledge (*Jnana Joga*), love (*Bhakti Yoga*), work (*Karma Yoga*), and psychological experimentation (*Raja Yoga*).[†] In the tradition of the goddess of wisdom Vajravaradri, who drives away evil spirits such as depression, mental health professionals in India treating depression regularly recruit religious wisdom to enhance support and a sense of direction.[‡]

---

[*] Almeida (2004, p. 82).

[†] Sharma (2000, pp. 341–343).

[‡] Patil (2003).

Muslims

Muslims see everything in life, including hardship, as coming from God. Surrender to God is the principal means of achieving contentment, and protection from depression. Expression of conflict, negative emotion, and introspection are poorly accepted in some Muslim cultures[*] where stigma remains an obstacle to recognizing and treating depression.[†] Not surprisingly, Loewenthal[‡] found that Muslims surveyed were more likely than individuals of other faiths to believe in the efficacy of religious activities such as prayer and reading the Koran for depression, were more likely to say they would use such activities, and least likely to seek professional intervention such as psychotherapy for depression. Family and community support, which are centrally important in many Muslin cultures, often take the place of professional counseling.

Atheists

In contrast to many religious individuals, secularists generally have less difficulty accepting a biomedical model of depression as a disease, and more difficulty seeing ultimate questions as relevant to mental health treatment.[§] They more often see suicide as a potentially rational choice[¶] consistent with the logic of atheist

---

[*] Hedayat-Diba (2000, p. 304).
[†] Nasir and Al-Qutob (2005).
[‡] Loewenthal et al. (2001).
[§] Saeed and Grant (2004, p. 139).
[¶] Emanuel (2002).

existentialists such as Sartre, Camus, and Beckett. Freud's use of a physician's services to end his own life is a familiar example.

As we can see from this brief review, depression is a challenge to most religious traditions, since it undermines the meaning, hope, identity, and affirming relationship to ultimate authority that they represent. Most believers acknowledge that serious depression warrants professional treatment. However, the relationship between milder depression and faith is often nuanced. Some see feelings of guilt and feelings of personal inadequacy as reasons to believe, or to practice one's faith more consistently. Or they may regard periods of doubt and struggle as important in the process of growth to spiritual maturity. At the same time, faith traditions offer a vision of reality that contradicts the darkness of depression. Some, such as Christianity and Buddhism, offer spiritual practices that address traumatic and characterological vulnerabilities to depression, and Hinduism tailors its approaches to individual temperaments. While atheists are more likely to view depression as an illness than a failure of adaptation to reality, their philosophies of life also influence existential choices important in depression, such as what makes life worth living, and when it should end.

Clinical Implications

What is the clinical significance of the relationship we have explored between depression and the soul? Consider briefly some ways that spirituality can be a resource or an exacerbating factor in depression, and that depression can enhance or interfere with a patient's spirituality.

Spirituality Can Worsen Depression

When the spiritual answers by which depressed individuals deal with existential concerns fail, their struggles with identity, hope, meaning/purpose, morality, and connection with authority can become overwhelming. An individual's world view or immature level of spiritual development may be unable to sustain his identity through illness.

> A 70-year-old Unitarian minister with progressive pancreatic cancer asked his caregivers to let him die. He explained that rather than believing in "someone out there," he had always committed himself to helping others. Without being able to serve, he had lost his sense of himself and felt unworthy to be served.

The failure of a pastor or a religious parent to provide needed care and protection can undermine hope. As an example, a woman in her twenties with an abusive childhood who had became a born-again Christian came for treatment of depression after she learned that her pastor had attempted to seduce her friend. Her despair was worse because she had begun to doubt God's protection.

Emergence from a high-demand religious community can result in a loss of purpose and meaning.

> After several attempts, a carpenter in his forties left a cult and saw a therapist for depression. He had joined the family-oriented group after being widowed in his twenties with two young children, attracted by its vision of worldwide harmony, but became disenchanted by the group's practice of soliciting new converts through sex.

Guilt can weigh more heavily on depressed individuals when experienced in religious terms. A conviction that God is judging them harshly can be worsened if their spiritual leaders treat their depression as a lack of faith, or expect them to simply repudiate a problematic behavior. For example, a conservative priest refused communion to a woman hospitalized for cancer because she was divorced. Her feelings of shame and embarrassment revived earlier rejections and made her feel she was unacceptable to God.

Suffering can strain an individual's relationship with God to the breaking point.[*] For example, a person whose faith has been based on God as protector can feel his faith shattered and can feel unloved by God.

> An architect in his forties became tearful and unable to focus on work after his wife developed metastatic breast cancer. He cried to God for healing so that she would be there for him and their daughter, but eventually lost hope that he was being heard. Although not an observant Jew, he had a sense of trust in God before his wife's illness, and now felt abandoned by him.

---

[*] Peteet (2001).

SPIRITUALITY CAN HELP DEPRESSION

On the other hand, a robust spirituality can ameliorate depression by providing answers to pressing existential concerns, and by helping to move the sufferer beyond self-absorbed isolation.

Knowing who one is within a transcendent context can help ground a sense of identity. Twelve Step Programs such as Alcoholics Anonymous, which describe themselves as spiritual, offer a person who has lost everything a redefinition of himself in relation to a Higher Power—as a recovering alcoholic, and a person capable of change, growth, and of helping others.[*] The graduate student in her twenties (described later in this chapter, see pp. 60–61) who had been anorectic recovered a sense of herself as loveable through a conviction that God loved her, mediated by her faith community.

Hope can come from knowing where one is within a larger context, and where one is going after death. But individuals who have lost the capacity to trust also need a spirituality that will realistically address their pain and doubt.

> A 27-year-old social worker with a history of childhood sexual abuse cut herself during episodes of feeling numb and hopeless, many triggered by her work with patients. Therapy involved months of establishing trust in her therapist, and in God, whom she had asked for healing. Several approaches helped her to integrate her spirituality and her experience of trauma. These included honest prayer with her pastor, and with members of a weekly prayer group; having friends

---

[*] Peteet (1993).

from church accompany her from therapy sessions when she did not feel safe alone; and after she stabilized, participating in a program focused on religiously based emotional healing.

Spirituality can help individuals to find meaning in their suffering as purifying, redemptive, or broadening. Mindfulness can enhance this process,* and other spiritual practices including prayer, worship, and service can help depressed individuals maintain a connection to the larger world.

An atheist can find meaning or connection to something larger in other ways.

A 50-year-old, bright administrator with borderline personality disorder often felt disrespected at work and periodically declared her intention to kill herself because her life was meaningless. As an atheist she had always regarded the spiritual practices of faith communities absurd, but she found a sustaining sense of space, historical perspective, and a shared experience of beauty in Renaissance literature classes.

Religious traditions offer ways of finding forgiveness for moral failures, as well as of developing morally admirable traits or virtues. Clinicians can often help patients examine their resistance to accepting the forgiveness that their spiritual tradition offers. They can also help those in spiritual programs such as Alcoholics Anonymous to take steps that help them ask for it from others, make amends, and serve.

---

* Segal et al. (2002).

The impact of religiously mediated forgiveness on delusional guilt is more likely to be indirect.

> A 65-year-old Protestant minister approaching retirement developed an agitated depression marked by the conviction that he had committed the unforgivable sin and was destined for hell. Efforts to engage him in theological discussion were ineffective, but encouragement by his family and church friends enabled him to accept antidepressant and antipsychotic medication, supportive psychotherapy, and help in planning for his retirement.

Depressed individuals who feel estranged from God often benefit from help engaging spiritual resources.

> A 35-year-old mother of two with chronic depression became more aware of her limitations as a parent, and the criticism she had received from her judgmental mother and demanding, largely absent father. She also reported that God seemed more distant and forbidding. After she accepted her therapist's suggestion to approach her pastor with her concerns, she and the pastor had an open and emotional encounter, during which the pastor's prayer helped her to feel more accepted by her pastor and by God.

DEPRESSION CAN ENHANCE SPIRITUALITY

Depression can stimulate interest in, or deepen, spirituality by enhancing awareness of one's limitations, by signaling that all is not well in the world, and by intensifying one's search for God.

Depressed individuals are more aware of their failures, the limits of their control, and the inadequacy of their previous sources of satisfaction. As a result, they are often more open to help from resources outside themselves. A number of its sufferers have written about what depression has taught them.[*,†] For example, Eric Wilson, in his *Against Happiness: In Praise of Melancholy*,[‡] refers to the melancholy that "generates a deep feeling in regard to this same anxiety, a turbulence of heart that results in an active questioning of the status quo, a perpetual longing to create new ways of being and seeing." Kathleen Norris[§] summarizes the wisdom of ancient mystics by saying, "Only when we admit we have 'no way' do we have a hope of finding one. Out of what seems desolate a new faith can arise, a certainty that is not subject to changes in moods or feelings, or the vicissitudes of life" (p. 263).

Step One of the Twelve Steps involves admitting one's powerlessness, and religious traditions recognize this as an important point of entry. Awareness that suffering is inevitable, Buddhists point out, is the first step toward enlightenment. Many of the Psalms of David begin with his despair. Jesus taught, "Blessed are those who weep."

---

[*] Crafton (2009).
[†] Smith (1997).
[‡] Wilson (2008).
[§] Norris (2008).

Depression-induced turning outside for help may be impulsive, as when Solomon* found himself praying in desperation to God he "was not sure I believed in." It may also initiate a process leading toward spiritual insight and maturity, as described by Greenspan in her book, *Healing Through the Dark Emotions: The Wisdom of Grief, Fear and Despair.*[†]

> A 50-year-old salesman had abused alcohol and cocaine until developing cancer of the mouth and being told by his oncologist that he had to stop. Frightened and depressed, he agreed to see the hospital psychiatrist and began to attend AA. A few years later, he attributed his sobriety and improved mood to his spirituality, the central feature of which he named as daily reliance on his "Higher Power."

Pain can increase empathy, and guilt may make depressed individuals more aware of what is wrong with the world. If not immobilizing, this heightened sensitivity can stimulate and help sustain altruistic spiritual commitments. Some believe that Abraham Lincoln consciously coped with major depression by actively cultivating a sense of purpose and a determination to contribute substantially to society.[‡]

> A chronically depressed college student with anorexia nervosa was drawn to a religious group on campus because the members seemed happier than she. After joining, her empathy for the unhappiness of

---

* Solomon (2001).
† Greenspan (2003).
‡ Shenk (2005).

others led her to intern as a hospital chaplain and to consider either nursing school or seminary as ways of fulfilling her sense of calling.

Although struggles with God over suffering and that of the world can end in despair and distance, they can also deepen the relationship. Among the best known descriptions of this process is St. John of the Cross's *Dark Night of the Soul*,[*,†] considered in greater detail in the next chapter.

> A divorced woman in her fifties, whose depressions during her twenties and thirties had led to repeated hospitalizations, psychotherapy, and medication, stabilized without treatment for many years after she underwent a religious conversion. She later explained that her desire for a close relationship had been largely satisfied by God. When she returned with depression following a number of losses, she also began to search for a new spiritual director.

Depression Can Undermine Spirituality

Finally, serious depression can impair an individual's capacity to feel, think, and act in ways that normally characterize his spirituality. He may lack access to positive emotions such as trust, hope, love, or joy. His thinking may be negative, cynical, hopeless, nihilistic, or even psychotic. And he may be unable to initiate or tolerate close relationships. Loss of a valued spiritual life can contribute to further depression and spiritual despair.

---

[*] John of the Cross (1990).
[†] May (2004).

A semiretired physician became depressed following a diagnosis of prostate cancer. He had been a perfectionistic, somewhat obsessional man respected in his congregation for his knowledge of and well-considered perspective on the scriptures. After becoming depressed, he ruminated over having lost his faith and was unmoved by counter-arguments from members of his congregation.

In many cases, depression and spirituality interact in more complex ways.

A single accountant in her fifties came for treatment because of intermittent depressions marked by tearfulness, withdrawal from others, and feelings of abandonment. As an only child of a troubled marriage, she had found herself caring for her parents from a young age and had continued to do so after they divorced. When they died, she became more active in her Protestant church, but continued to feel lonely and struggled with God over why he had not provided her with a life partner. In treatment she came to recognize that her pattern of putting the needs of others ahead of her own had left her resentful that no one was actively providing for her. On one hand, she experienced God as a constant source of comfort and her church activities as sources of connection and affirmation. On the other, she also felt disappointed by God for not protecting her from loneliness, which contributed to her depression and passivity.

In this chapter we have considered some of the ways that depressed individuals can experience spiritual distress in their search for answers to existential questions in the domains of identity, hope, meaning/purpose, morality, and autonomy/relationship to authority. We have briefly reviewed research evidence that spiritual and religious involvement can help depression, as well as some of the approaches offered by major traditional world views. Finally, we have highlighted the often complex and dynamic ways in which depression and spirituality can interact. In the next chapter we consider a framework for assessing and distinguishing depression and spiritual distress in their various forms, and for incorporating these into a diagnostic formulation that can serve as a basis for a comprehensive plan of care and treatment.

References

A View on Buddhism: Depression. (2004). Retrieved from http://buddhism.kalachakranet.org/depression.html; accessed December 15, 2009.

Adams, J.E. (1972). *Competent to Counsel.* Grand Rapids: Baker Book House.

Almeida, R. (2004). *The Politics of Mourning: Grief Management in Cross-Cultural Fiction.* Madison, NJ: Fairleigh Dickinson University Press.

Azhar, M.Z., & Varma, S.L. (1995). Religious psychotherapy in depressive patients. *Psychother Psychosom,* 63, 165–168.

Bartlett, S.J., Piedmont, R., Bilderback, A., Matsumoto, A.K., & Bathon, J.M. (2003). Spirituality, well-being, and quality of life in people with rheumatoid arthritis. *Arthritis Rheum,* 49, 778–783.

Beck, A.T., Steer, R.A., Kovacs, M., & Garrison, B. (1985). Hopelessness and eventual suicide: A 10-year prospective study of patients hospitalized with suicidal ideation. *Am J Psychiatry,* 142(5), 559–563.

Blazer, D.G. (1998). *Freud Versus God: How Psychiatry Lost Its Soul and Christianity Lost Its Mind.* Downers Grove, IL: InterVarsity Press.

Blazer, D.G. (2005). *The Age of Melancholy: "Major Depression" and Its Social Origins.* New York: Routledge.

Boscaglia, N., Clarke, D.M., Jobling, T.W., & Quinn, M.A. (2005). The contribution of spirituality and spiritual coping to anxiety and depression in women with a recent diagnosis of gynecological cancer. *Int J Gynecol Cancer,* 15, 755–761.

Bufford, R.K., Paloutzian, R.F., & Ellison, C.W. (1991). Norms for the Spiritual Well-Being Scale. *J Psychology and Theology,* 19, 56–70.

Carrico, A.W., Ironson, G., Antoni, M.H., Lechner, S.C., Duran, R.E., Kumar, M. et al. (2006). A path model of the effects of spirituality on depressive symptoms and 24-h urinary-free cortisol in HIV-positive persons. *J Psychosom Res,* 61(1), 51–58.

Coleman, C.L., & Holzemer, W.L. (1999). Spirituality, psychological well-being, and HIV symptoms for African Americans living with HIV disease. *J Assoc Nurses AIDS Care,* 10(1), 42–50.

Conroy, T. (2004). Depression is a 'spiritual trial.' *Catholic Medical Quarterly* (Vol. February, 2004, pp. 1–2).

Cooper, L.A., Brown, C., Vu, H.T., Ford, D.E., & Powe, N.R. (2001). How important is intrinsic spirituality in depression care? A comparison of white and African American primary care patients. *J Gen Intern Med,* 16, 634–638.

Crafton, B.C. (2009). *Jesus Wept: When Faith and Depression Meet.* San Francisco: Jossey-Bass.

Cunningham, J., Sirey, J.A., & Bruce, M.L. (2007). Matching services to patients' beliefs about depression in Dublin, Ireland. *Psychiatr Serv,* 58(5), 696–699.

Daaleman, T.P., Frey, B.B., Wallace, D., & Studenski, S.A. (2002). Spirituality Index of Well-Being Scale: Development and testing of a new measure. *J Fam Pract,* 51, 952.

Daaleman, T.P., & Kaufman, J.S. (2006). Spirituality and depressive symptoms in primary care outpatients. *South Med J,* 99, 1340–1344.

Durkheim, E. (1951). *Suicide, a Study in Sociology.* Glencoe, IL: Free Press.

Emanuel, E.J. (2002). Euthanasia and physician-assisted suicide: A review of the empirical data from the United States. *Arch Intern Med,* 162, 142–152.

Foster, R.J. (1978). *Celebration of Discipline: The Path to Spiritual Growth.* San Francisco: Harper & Row.

Fry, P.S. (2000). Religious involvement, spirituality and personal meaning for life: Existential predictors of psychological wellbeing in community-residing and institutional care elders. *Aging and Mental Health,* 4, 375–387.

Gillum, T.L., Sullivan, C.M., & Bybee, D.I. (2006). The importance of spirituality in the lives of domestic violence survivors. *Violence Against Women,* 12, 240–250.

Gitlin, T. (2001). *Media Unlimited: How the Torrent of Images and Sounds Overwhelms Our Lives* (1st ed.). New York: Metropolitan Books.

Givens, J.L., Houston, T.K., Van Voorhees, B.W., Ford, D.E., & Cooper, L.A. (2007). Ethnicity and preferences for depression treatment. *Gen Hosp Psychiatry,* 29, 182–191.

Greenspan, M. (2003). *Healing Through the Dark Emotions: The Wisdom of Grief, Fear and Despair.* Boston: Shambhala Publications, Inc.

Hallowell, E. (2007). *CrazyBusy—Overstretched, Overbooked and About to Snap! Strategies for Coping in a World Gone ADD.* New York: Ballantine Books.

Hedayat-Diba, Z. (2000). Psychotherapy with Muslims. In P.S. Richards & A.E. Bergin (Eds.), *Handbook of Psychotherapy and Religious Diversity* (pp. 518). Washington, DC: American Psychological Association.

Herman, J.L. (1997). *Trauma and Recovery* (Rev. ed.). New York: Basic Books.

Hopkins, G.M. (1918) Carrion comfort. In *Poems.* London: Humphrey Milford.

Jackson, B. (1999). *The Quest for the Radical Middle: A History of the Vineyard.* Cape Town, South Africa: Vineyard International Publishing.

James, W. (1902). The Varieties of Religious Experience; a Study in Human Nature; being the Gifford Lectures on Natural Religion delivered at Edinburgh in 1901–1902. New York: Longmans Green.

John of the Cross. (1990). *Dark Night of the Soul* (Peers, E.A., & Silverio De Santa Teresa, P., Trans.). New York: Image Books Doubleday.

Jones, J.W. (2003). *The Mirror of God: Christian Faith as Spiritual Practice.* New York: Palgrave Macmillan.

Kaplan, K.J., & Schwartz, M.B. (2000). From tragedy to therapy: A psychology of hope. *Journal of Psychology and Judaism* 24, 159–164.

Karp, D.A. (1996). *Speaking of Sadness: Depression, Disconnection, and the Meanings of Illness.* New York: Oxford University Press.

Kaye, J., & Raghavan, S.K. (2002). Spirituality in disability and illness. *J Religion and Health* 41, 231–243.

Kleinman, A. (1988). *Rethinking Psychiatry: From Cultural Category to Personal Experience.* New York, London: Free Press; Collier Macmillan.

Koenig, H.G. (2005). *Faith and Mental Health: Religious Resources for Healing.* West Conshohocken, PA: Templeton Foundation Press.

Koenig, H.G., McCullough, M.E., & Larson, D.B. (2001). *Handbook of Religion and Health.* Oxford; New York: Oxford University Press.

Koenig, H.G., Pargament, K.I., & Nielsen, J. (1998). Religious coping and health status in medically ill hospitalized older adults. *J Nerv Ment Dis,* 186, 513–521.

Kroll, J., Egan, E., Erickson, P., Carey, K., & Johnson, M. (2004). Moral conflict, religiosity, and neuroticism in an outpatient sample. *J Nerv Ment Dis,* 192, 682–688.

Krupski, T.L., Kwan, L., Fink, A., Sonn, G.A., Maliski, S., & Litwin, M.S. (2006). Spirituality influences health related quality of life in men with prostate cancer. *Psycho-oncology,* 15, 121–131.

LaHaye, T.F. (1974). *How to Win Over Depression.* Grand Rapids, MI: Zondervan Pub. House.

Levenson, M.R., Aldwin, C.M., & Yancura, L. (2006). Positive emotional change: Mediating effects of forgiveness and spirituality. *Explore (NY),* 2, 498–508.

Loewenthal, K.M., Cinnirella, M., Evdoka, G., & Murphy, P. (2001). Faith conquers all? Beliefs about the role of religious factors in coping with depression among different cultural-religious groups in the UK. *Br J Med Psychol,* 74, 293–303.

Maselko, J., Gilman, S.E., & Buka., S. (2008). Religious service attendance and spiritual well-being are differentially associated with risk of major depression. http://journals.cambridge.org/action/display Abstract?fromPage=online&aid=2384452; retrieved March 7, 2009.

May, G.G. (2004). *The Dark Night of the Soul: A Psychiatrist Explores the Connection Between Darkness and Spiritual Growth* (1st ed.). San Francisco: Harper.

McClain, C.S., Rosenfeld, B., & Breitbart, W. (2003). Effect of spiritual well-being on end-of-life despair in terminally-ill cancer patients. *Lancet,* 361, 1603–1607.

McCoubrie, R.C., & Davies, A.N. (2006). Is there a correlation between spirituality and anxiety and depression in patients with advanced cancer? *Support Care Cancer,* 14, 379–385.

McCullough, M.E., & Larson, D.B. (1999). Religion and depression: A review of the literature. *Twin Res,* 2, 126–136.

Meadow, M.J. (1989). Four stages of spiritual experience: A comparison of the Ignatian Exercises and Jungian psychotherapy. *Pastoral Psychology,* 37, 172–191.

Meissner, W.W. (1999). *To the Greater Glory: A Psychological Study of Ignatian Spirituality.* Milwaukee, WI: Marquette University Press.

Nasir, L.S., & Al-Qutob, R. (2005). Barriers to the diagnosis and treatment of depression in Jordan. A nationwide qualitative study. *J Am Board Fam Pract,* 18, 125–131.

Nelson, C.J., Rosenfeld, B., Breitbart, W., & Galietta, M. (2002). Spirituality, religion, and depression in the terminally ill. *Psychosomatics,* 43, 213–220.

Norris, K. (2008). *Acedia and Me: A Marriage, Monks and a Writer's Life.* New York: Riverhead Books.

Pargament, K.I. (1997). *The Psychology of Religion and Coping: Theory, Research, Practice.* New York: Guilford Press.

Patil, B. (2003). The meaning of depression and malaise seen from the perspective of Hinduism. Pontifcium Consilium Pro PastoraliValetudinus Cura XVIII International Conference.

Peteet, J.R. (1993). A closer look at the role of a spiritual approach in addictions treatment. *J Subst Abuse Treat,* 10, 263–267.

Peteet, J.R. (2001). Putting suffering into perspective: Implications of the patient's world view. *J Psychother Pract Res,* 10, 187–192.

Peterman, A.H., Fitchett, G., Brady, M.J., Hernandez, L., & Cella, D. (2002). Measuring spiritual well-being in people with cancer: The functional assessment of chronic illness therapy—Spiritual Well-Being Scale (FACIT-Sp). *Ann Behav Med, 24*, 49–58.

Piedmont, R.L. (1999). Does spirituality represent the sixth factor of personality? Spiritual transcendence and the five-factor model. *J Personality* 67, 985–1013.

Probst, L.R., Ostrom, R., Watkins, P., Dean, T., & Mashburn, D. (1992). Comparative efficacy of religious and nonreligious cognitive therapy for the treatment of depression in religious individuals. *J Consulting and Counseling Psychology,* 60, 94–103.

Rambo, L.R. (1993). *Understanding Religious Conversion.* New Haven, CT: Yale University Press.

Saeed, S.A., & Grant, R.L. (2004). Atheists and agnostics. In A.J. Josephson & J.R. Peteet (Eds.), *Handbook of Spirituality and World View in Clinical Practice* (1st ed., p. 168). Arlington, VA: American Psychiatric Publishing, Inc.

Segal, Z.V., Williams, J.M. G., & Teasdale, J.D. (2002). *Mindfulness-Based Cognitive Therapy for Depression: A New Approach to Preventing Relapse.* New York: Guilford Press.

Sharma, A.R. (2000). Psychotherapy with Hindus. In P.S. Richards & A.E. Bergin (Eds.), *Handbook of Psychotherapy and Religious Diversity* (p. 518). Washington, DC: American Psychological Association.

Shenk, J.W. (2005). *Lincoln's Melancholy: How Depression Challenged a President and Fueled His Greatness.* Boston: Houghton Mifflin Co.

Shuman, J.J., & Meador, K.G. (2003). *Heal Thyself: Spirituality, Medicine, and the Distortion of Christianity.* New York: Oxford University Press.

Smith, J. (1997). *Where the Roots Reach for Water: A Personal & Natural History of Melancholia.* New York: North Point Press.

Smith, T.B., McCullough, M.E., & Poll, J. (2003). Religiousness and depression: Evidence for a main effect and the moderating influence of stressful life events. *Psychol Bull,* 129, 614–636.

Solomon, A. (2001). *The Noonday Demon: An Atlas of Depression.* New York: Scribner.

Springer, M.B., Newman, A., Weaver, A.J., Siritsky, N., Linderblatt, C., Flannelly, K.J. et al. (2003). Spirituality, depression, and loneliness among Jewish seniors residing in New York City. *J Pastoral Care Counsel,* 57(3), 305–318.

Styron, W. (1990). *Darkness Visible: A Memoir of Madness.* New York: Random House.

Toffler, A. (1970). *Future Shock.* New York: Random House.

Weissman, M.M., Markowitz, J.C., & Klerman, G.L. (2007). *Clinician's Quick Guide to Interpersonal Psychotherapy.* Oxford; New York: Oxford University Press.

Willard, D. (1998). *The Spirit of the Disciplines: Understanding How God Changes Lives.* New York: Harper Collins.

Wilson, E.G. (2008). *Against Happiness: In Praise of Melancholy.* New York: Farrar, Straus and Giroux, p. 8.

Wink, P., Dillon, M., & Larsen, B. (2005). Religion as moderator of the depression-health connection: Findings from a longitudinal study. *Research on Aging,* 27, 197–220.

Yisra\U+02be\eli, Y. a. (1981). Bet òKarlin Sòtolin: Peraòkim bemasekhet òhayehem shel admo"re ha-shoshelet òve-°iyunim bamishnatam ha-òhasidit. Tel-Aviv: òKeren Ya°aòkov òve-Raòhel.

3 Differential Diagnosis, Assessment, and Formulation

If you don't know where you are going to, you will end up somewhere else.

Lewis Carroll

What distinguishes depression from a spiritual problem? When both are present, how can one assess the relationship between them? Where do spiritual problems belong in a clinical formulation?

To explore these questions, in this chapter I take a finer-grained look at the range of conditions that are marked by a lowered mood. These include familiar diagnostic categories of depression, as well as distressing existential and spiritual conditions with which they are sometimes confused: melancholic, bipolar, and psychotic depression; depression associated with personality, addiction, and trauma; adjustment disorder; prolonged grief; demoralization; angst; guilt; the "dark night of the soul"; and ordinary unhappiness. Others, such as medically caused depression (for example, by hypothyroidism) and socially conditioned emotional distress,[*] would belong in a complete list.

Assessing a patient for these conditions involves active listening, screening, and deeper inquiry. Formulating the patient's case involves understanding how the condition arose, the role it continues to play in the patient's life, and what resources are most likely to help him to move forward.

Differential Diagnosis

In 1973, Akiskal and McKinney amassed a large body of evidence in support of a unitary hypothesis according to which the depressive syndrome is a "psychobiological final pathway."[†] Its symptoms are familiar: persistent feelings of sadness, difficulty concentrating, indecisiveness, hopelessness, pessimism, guilt or worthlessness, fatigue, lack of energy and initiative, an impaired capacity for enjoyment, disturbances of sleep and appetite, and thoughts of death or suicide. Their conception came to dominate the field and shaped the category of Major Depressive Disorder in the *Diagnostic and Statistical Manual* (DSM). It also fit popular descriptions of depression by sufferers such as Solomon (*The Noonday Demon: An Atlas of Depression*[‡]) and Styron (*Darkness Visible: A Memoir of*

---

[*] Blazer (2005).

[†] Akiskal and McKinney (1973, p. 286).

[‡] Solomon (2001).

Madness[*]), whose individual illnesses seemed to take on a life of their own, eventually depriving them of rational perspective and a sense of control.

However, a number of investigators have questioned whether this model may be overly simplistic. Parker[†] has suggested that depression without psychomotor (melancholic) or psychotic features is better regarded as a spectrum of disordered responses to life that are "induced and/or maintained by predisposing factors." Kendler et al.[‡] have similarly proposed a model of major depression that is etiologically diverse, "influenced by risk factors from multiple domains that act in developmental time." Horwitz and Wakefield[§] go further to suggest that psychiatry's system of classification has "transformed normal sorrow into depressive disorder." And from a therapeutic point of view, Schatzberg[¶] has called on clinicians to move beyond symptom control to manage the underlying vulnerabilities that contribute to recurrent depression.

If we take a stress diathesis perspective, we can see that several conditions confer a vulnerability to a depressed mood, and that they differ in their etiologies as well as in their therapeutic implications. They may also have different spiritual implications.

---

[*] Styron (1990).
[†] Parker (2000, p. 1199).
[‡] Kendler et al. (2006, p. 115).
[§] Horwitz and Wakefield (2007).
[¶] Schatzberg (2006).

Melancholia and Psychotic Depression

The term melancholia, derived from the Greek words for black bile (melaina chole), has historical origins in the humoral theory of depressive illness. In the technical psychiatric sense, melancholic features of major depression include prominent disturbances in sleep, appetite, energy, and the capacity for enjoyment. Studies have shown melancholic depression to be relatively independent of environmental influence—episodes may be externally precipitated, but often do not appear to be.[*,†] Both its vegetative and psychological symptoms (e.g., self-blame) are typically less responsive to interpersonal than to somatic treatments, such as medication or electroconvulsive therapy (ECT).

Psychotic forms of major depression involve hallucinations, or delusions, for example of guilt or worthlessness. These can take religious form, as in the case of the pastor in Chapter 2, who believed he had lost his salvation. As with melancholia, interpersonal interventions are typically less effective than biological treatments. Religious concerns can present important obstacles to accepting antidepressant and antipsychotic medication if a patient views his condition as a judgment from God. The pastor mentioned above objected, "I'm not crazy—God just has it in for me."

---

[*] Biro and Till (1989).
[†] Marcos and Salamero (1990).

BIPOLAR DEPRESSION

Bipolar depression like melancholia often presents with a genetic load, is relatively independent of life events, and is more responsive to somatic than interpersonal treatments. Bipolar patients may also resist accepting needed medication on religious grounds, although religious delusions are more common in the manic phase. When depressed, bipolar individuals who recognize that their spiritual experience during mania was psychotic may be embarrassed and hesitant to reengage with their faith.

> A 30-year-old Protestant mother of two discontinued her mood stabilizers during pregnancy. She required hospitalization after delivery when she became sleepless, agitated, and preoccupied with convincing others that God was communicating with her in a special way. Later, when depressed, she found it difficult to trust her spiritual beliefs, which had previously been an important resource and source of support.

While medication is centrally important in stabilizing the lives of such patients, the spectrum concept of mood disorders has led to growing concern about overdiagnosis of bipolar disorder on the basis of relatively mild "mood instability" or transient "mood swings."* The result can be that inexperienced clinicians may reinforce the identity of patients as "bipolar," with a focus on biological explanations and solutions to the neglect of other factors, such as those we consider below.

---
* Hutto (2001).

DEPRESSION RELATED TO PERSONALITY

The category of depressive personality, or chronic characterological depression has never been incorporated into the DSM.[*] However, as many as 20 to 50 percent of inpatients and 50 to 85 percent of outpatients with a current major depressive disorder or dysthymia have an associated personality disorder.[†,‡,§] The incidence is considerably higher in nonmelancholic, nonbipolar[¶] patients, and in those with late onset depression.[**] Many dynamically oriented clinicians believe that character-based emotional inhibition predisposes individuals to depression by turning their aggression inward.

To test a stress diathesis model of personality contributing to depression, a number of studies have examined whether dependent (or "sociotropic") and autonomous (or self-critical) personality types predispose individuals to depression when subject to interpersonal loss or failure to achieve. Noting that this research has been inconclusive, Coyne and Whiffen[††] have suggested that a better model may need to take into account social context, resources, experience with depression, and the interaction among these factors and personal functioning.

---

[*] Phillips et al. (1990).
[†] Shea et al. (1990).
[‡] Sanderson et al. (1992).
[§] Corruble et al. (1996).
[¶] Charney et al. (1981).
[**] Fava et al. (1996).
[††] Coyne and Whiffen (1995).

An alternative hypothesis is that personality-related vulnerability to depression, rather than being attributable to distinct personality styles, represents a common factor such as neuroticism.[*] Peter Kramer's[†] observation that agents such as Prozac seem to alter the personalities of individuals who have been subtly dysphoric for most of their lives is bolstered by the finding of Fava et al.[‡] that successful treatment of outpatients with major depression using fluoxetine reduced the frequency of most personality disorder diagnoses. Although the relationship between personality and dysthymia remains unclear[§] the authors concluded that the effects of serotonin reuptake inhibitors (SRIs) on baseline emotional reactivity may be the means by which they protect against depression in these cases.

> A 40-year-old pastor's wife and mother of three described having always been a lifelong "worrier" prone to recurring periods of irritability and low spirits. Her family urged her to seek professional evaluation, and she saw a psychiatrist who prescribed an SRI. She was initially reluctant to take a medication rather than rely on prayer and faith, but after a few weeks found that most of the variability in her mood had disappeared.

Cloninger et al.[¶] found the character dimension of self-transcendence (indicated by being intuitive, judicious, spiritual)

---

[*] Kendler et al. (1993).
[†] Kramer (1997).
[‡] Fava et al. (1994).
[§] Phillips et al. (1998).
[¶] Cloninger et al. (1993).

to be inversely related to the incidence of personality disorder. Interestingly, Borg et al.[*] using positron emission tomography (PET) to study the relationship between brain 5-HT 1A receptor density and personality in normal male subjects found a positive correlation only with the spiritual acceptance subscale of the self-transcendence dimension. The authors suggest that the serotonin system may serve as a biological basis for spiritual experience. Could self-transcendence, perhaps mediated by serotonin, help protect against depression?[†]

> A 50-year-old office worker with long-standing feelings of victimization, intense and inevitably disappointing relationships with bosses, and angry moods also complained of feeling depressed much of the time. An SRI seemed to modulate her mood and her pessimistic view of the world to only a limited degree. Her therapist focused on helping her to recognize the distorted assumptions and unrealistic assumptions that kept her repeating self-defeating and disappointing encounters. This approach was somewhat more helpful, but she continued to feel empty and cynical. He then explored with her what might take her beyond her negative self-absorption. She had no use for religion, but was able at times to lose herself in jewelry making and drawing, and to enjoy befriending an elderly neighbor.

To encourage this capacity for transcending her focus on herself, her psychiatrist might also have recommended that this patient consider mindfulness exercises, or dialectical behavior therapy (DBT).

---

[*] Borg et al. (2003).
[†] Cloninger (2006).

DEPRESSION RELATED TO ADDICTION

The presence of drug abuse is estimated to increase the risk for depression almost five times.[*] Cigarette smokers have almost twice the risk average of developing depression.[†] Alcohol dependence imposes physical, emotional, social, and spiritual burdens that contribute to depression. Furthermore, many individuals self-medicate depression.[‡]

A recent meta-analysis of treatment for patients with both depression and alcohol or other drug dependence showed that antidepressant medication showed a modest beneficial effect, but was not a stand-alone treatment. The authors recommended concurrent treatment of both conditions.[§] Arguably the most successful approach to addiction, Twelve Step Programs, which define themselves as spiritual, address addicts' problems in the areas of identity, integrity, interdependence, and an inner life.[¶]

> A 19-year-old college student with a history of a tumultuous relationship with his mother and variable moods began to binge on alcohol and cocaine. When his primary care physician presented him with evidence of alcoholic hepatitis, he reluctantly agreed to visit an Alcoholics Anonymous (AA) meeting. After attending meetings regularly for some time, he became sober, obtained a sponsor, and began to recognize the ways he had been acting impulsively and in

---

[*] Regier et al. (1990).
[†] Breslau et al. (1998).
[‡] Schuckit (2006).
[§] Nunes and Levin (2004).
[¶] Peteet (1993).

a "self-centered" way on his feelings. He described his spirituality—"working the program" (attending meetings, using his sponsor, and practicing the steps)—as the most important part of maintaining both his sobriety and his emotional equilibrium.

Depression Related to Trauma

Epidemiologic data suggests that posttraumatic stress disorder (PTSD) more than doubles the risk of depression.[*] In a study of a population of 211 trauma survivors recruited from an emergency room, 44 percent showed both conditions.[†] Some authors have suggested the presence of a dose–response relationship between trauma and depression.[‡,§] General stress could be one factor,[¶,**] but Judith Herman in *Trauma and Recovery*[††] has identified several specific ways that trauma damages the abilities of the individual to deal with the existential challenges of life: "Traumatized people suffer damage to the basic structures of the self. They lose their trust in themselves, in other people, and in God. Their self-esteem is assaulted by experiences of humiliation, guilt and helplessness. Their capacity for intimacy is compromised by intense and contradictory feelings of need and fear."

---

[*] Breslau et al. (1998).
[†] Shalev et al. (1998).
[‡] Mollica et al. (1998)
[§] Momartin et al. (2004).
[¶] O'Donnell et al. (2004).
[**] Campbell et al. (1997).
[††] Herman (1992, p. 56).

Differential Diagnosis, Assessment, and Formulation 81

> A 45-year-old separated teacher with chronic depression despaired of being able to have a normal relationship with a woman. He noted a tendency to become angry when a partner criticized him, and then unfaithful. Exploration revealed that he never felt he measured up to the expectations of his mother, who encouraged his father to punish him severely for minor infractions. When he was an adolescent she had invited a priest into her children's lives, who had sexually abused him. He had tried to conceal his feelings of anger, shame, and insecurity but they persisted, influencing his interactions both with women and with authorities. At times of crisis in such a relationship, he had felt despondent and hopeless, with transient suicidal ideation. As an adolescent, he made efforts to find solace through marijuana use and as an adult though developing a spiritual practice, but was hindered by painful memories of betrayal by the church.

As seen in this case, chronic abuse can contribute to depression. Feelings of being trapped and hopeless often in turn perpetuate abuse, for example of a battered woman. Such individuals sometimes report that developing spiritually has been important in beginning to heal and develop the capacity to take a stand.[*] However, spiritual authority can also be used to enforce abuse, as in the case of a religious 20-year-old who refused to report her father's sexual and physical assaults because her parents had used scripture to convince her that children should obey their parents. The importance of a caring and wise spiritual community in such cases is obvious.

---

[*] Senter and Caldwell (2002).

Prolonged Grief

The DSM-IV recognizes uncomplicated bereavement as a normal condition that may be worthy of clinical attention, and Wakefield et al.[*] have argued that this status should be extended to grief over other losses. But depression can also develop following loss.[†] To help distinguish complicated grief from depression, Prigerson et al.[‡] in a study of recent widows identified several symptoms that constitute a separate syndrome. Horowitz et al.[§] have since refined these to include the current experience more than a year after a loss of intense intrusive thoughts, pangs of severe emotion, distressing yearnings, feeling excessively alone and empty, excessively avoiding tasks reminiscent of the deceased, unusual sleep disturbances, and maladaptive levels of loss of interest in personal activities.

In attempting to explain the phenomenon of prolonged or complicated grief within a larger context, Neimeyer et al.[¶] suggest that adaptive attempts to find the meaning of loss take place at both individual and communal levels. At the level of the community, shared rituals, narrative practices, and local cultures offer ways to assimilate the significance of loss for survivors and to help regulate the emotional disruption of bereavement. At an

---

[*] Wakefield et al. (2007).
[†] Clayton et al. (1972).
[‡] Prigerson et al. (1995).
[§] Horowitz et al. (2003).
[¶] Neimeyer et al. (2002).

individual and interpersonal level, survivors struggle to integrate the loss into their existing "self-narratives." Viewed from this perspective, complicated grief reflects an inability to reconstruct a meaningful personal reality. The sufferer's world view is important to understand in determining if he has an adequate working model of the self and relationships.[*]

> A carpenter in his fifties was unusually close to his wife of 33 years before she died of breast cancer. Following her death, he was preoccupied, slept poorly, and began to use oxycodone to assuage his grief. He was emotional when reminded of their times together and found it difficult to reengage in work, or in coaching little league baseball. Although he was "not a religious person," he was a believer in God and found the service commemorating the first anniversary of her death an important and helpful way to review with their two children and friends what his life with his wife had meant.

As Neimeyer et al. also note, grief can prompt personal growth as well as despair, strengthening as well as decreasing the survivor's sense of meaning. Cassell[†] similarly emphasizes the role of meaning in dealing effectively with suffering, and Block[‡] describes the possibility of transcendence at the end of life.

DEMORALIZATION

Clinicians working in medical settings are familiar with the distinction between demoralization, or "giving up," and

---

[*] Peteet (2001).
[†] Cassell (1992).
[‡] Block (2001).

depression.[*,†] Demoralized patients stressed by the unexpectedness and uncertainty of hospitalization may show disturbances in sleep, appetite, and energy, and feel helpless, even passively suicidal in relation to the situation. However, they typically retain a responsive mood and, with the removal of adversity, rapidly regain hope and the capacity for enjoyment.[‡] This has led consultation liaison psychiatrists such as Slavney[§] to argue that demoralization is a normal, common condition that, like grief, should be designated a V code in the DSM.

Griffith and Gaby[‡] have identified several existential postures having healthier counterparts that are often adopted by demoralized individuals: confusion (vs. coherence), isolation (vs. communion), despair (vs. hope), helplessness (vs. agency), meaninglessness (vs. purpose), cowardice (vs. courage), and resentment (vs. gratitude). They suggest questions that clinicians can use to explore with both religious and nonreligious patients' potential sources of resilience. An example might be asking a patient who is feeling isolated, "Who really understands your situation?" or (for religious patients) "Do you feel the presence of God?"

> A 70-year-old semiretired professor with colon cancer that was causing progressive fatigue said he wanted to die because he could no longer be productive and in control. Explaining that he saw no way

---

[*] Clarke and Kissane (2002).
[†] Mangelli et al. (2005).
[‡] Griffith and Gaby (2005).
[§] Slavney (1999).

of returning to the person he had been, he asked, "What's the point of going on?"

A major source of resilience for this demoralized man was his relationships with family, who could help him see that he still mattered to them and valued the opportunity to care for him.

ADJUSTMENT DISORDER WITH DEPRESSED MOOD

Adjustment disorder, perhaps the diagnosis made most frequently by psychiatrists in the medical setting, refers to depressed and/or anxious symptoms out of proportion to a stressor such as an illness. As in the case of grief after a loss, these become understandable in relation to the meaning that it has for the individual. Viederman and Perry[*] in a classic paper highlight the role of a psychodynamic life narrative in treating a medically ill person with depression. For example, a narrative interview can help a man incapacitated by a heart attack who has always seen himself as a competent provider understand why he has so valued this role, how he is the same person although ill, and what he can still do to be the person he wants most to be.

> A 65-year-old retired doorman who required surgery for relapsed lung cancer was fatigued, discouraged about his progress, and sleeping poorly. He was particularly despondent about being unable to enjoy retirement with his wife.

---
[*] Viederman and Perry (1980).

Patients adjusting to serious medical illness are often experiencing spiritual distress.[*,†] For example, this patient, who had been a nominal Catholic for most of his life, became more religious after his diagnosis, but now felt angry and doubtful about God. Exploring the spiritual distress of such a patient can help him to clarify his expectations, grieve his loss, and identify what is most important to him in the time he has remaining.[‡]

Adjustment disorder is also common in outpatients whose hopes (conscious or not) have been disappointed.

> A 35-year-old Asian American executive presented with depressive symptoms as she approached two years of unemployment. She was the oldest child of immigrant parents who valued education and criticized her academic performance despite the fact that she excelled in both college and graduate school. Previous, similar episodes of indecision, self-doubt, poor energy, and social withdrawal coincided with points of transition, such as deciding what to do after graduation. She recalled being preoccupied by fears of doing the wrong thing, and wishing for her father's approval.
>
> An antidepressant helped to moderate these symptoms, and insight-oriented psychotherapy helped her understand them. After practicing in a conflict resolution workshop, she then experienced a "breakthrough" when she gently asked her father if his harsh criticisms reflected worries he had about her future. He tearfully revealed his hopes that she would become a leader in her field, and she responded with tears of her own. What followed was a closer, more open connection and improvement in her depression.

---

[*] Peteet (1985).

[†] Balboni et al. (2007).

[‡] Sulmasy (2006).

Religious individuals can similarly feel depressed when they feel that God has become disapproving and distant in ways that their parents were. Recognition of the patient's disappointed hopes can help the clinician to distinguish this phenomenon from guilt, and from the "dark night of the soul" (*vide infra*).

Angst

The Danish philosopher Soren Kierkegaard used the term *Angest* (Danish, meaning "dread") to denote the profound sense of insecurity experienced by human beings in the face of their freedom to act. Novelists (J.D. Salinger, Walker Percy, Kurt Vonnegut, and Don Delillo, to name a few) have since portrayed angst as pervasive in our culture. Psychiatrists including Rollo May,[*] Irving Yalom,[†] and Gerald May[‡] have called for recognizing existential distress as a legitimate focus of therapeutic attention.

In *The Sickness Unto Death*[§] Kierkegaard distinguished several manifestations of what he called "despair": a weak unwillingness to be oneself, a passive wish to be like someone else, an unconscious desire to believe that one lacks choice, and a defiant assertion of a self-destructive identity. He felt that an individual could show one or more of these in his struggle to be a self in relation to "the infinite." Kierkegaard's conception of

---

[*] May (1969).
[†] Yalom (1980).
[‡] May (1982).
[§] Kierkegaard (1849/1954).

existential anxiety was echoed a century later by the theologian Paul Tillich in his book *The Courage to Be*. The concept also overlaps to a large degree with the ancient concept of *acedia*, reviewed in depth by Kathleen Norris,[*] which she describes as literally "the absence of care," marked by apathy, boredom, torpor, or in moral terms, sloth. In attempting to distinguish acedia from what is usually understood as depression, she writes: "Having experienced both conditions, I think it is likely that much of the restless boredom, frantic escapism, commitment phobia, and enervating despair that plagues us today is the ancient demon of acedia in modern dress" (p. 3).

> After her mother's death from cancer, a college sophomore began abusing alcohol, then dropped out of school with vague hopes of becoming a manicurist. In the course of several brief attempts at work, she became dependent on benzodiazepines prescribed to treat free-floating anxiety. A psychiatrist who weaned her from these diagnosed a passive dependent personality, and prescribed an antidepressant, which had little effect on her sense of insecurity, indecisiveness, and frustration. After a time she stopped looking for work, explaining that she was unsure what she wanted to do. When her father stopped paying her bills, she began to depend on her boyfriend for money and applied for disability.

This patient intermittently suffered anxious and depressed moods that became the basis of her claim for disability, but these were symptomatic of a deeper problem. Her dread of

---
[*] Norris (2008).

becoming a responsible individual led her to feel powerless, to arrange being cared for by others, to define herself by her relationships with them, and to avoid self-awareness through her use of substances.

Kierkegaard saw the cure for the sickness unto death as faith, which he summarized in the following formula: "By relating itself to its own self and by willing to be itself, the self is grounded transparently in the Power which constituted it" (ibid., p. 262). His fierce attacks on "Christiandom" make clear that this relationship to the transcendent Power was not equivalent to religious belief, or even practice. It was instead a passionate spiritual stance. "A believer is surely a lover, yea, of all lovers the most in love" (ibid., p. 234).

The German theologian and martyr Dietrich Bonhoeffer[*] similarly contrasted "cheap" and "costly" grace.

> Cheap grace means grace sold on the market like a cheapjack's wares.... Cheap grace means a doctrine, a principle, a system. It means forgiveness of sins proclaimed as a general truth, the love of God taught as the Christian "conception" of God. An intellectual assent to that idea is held to be of itself sufficient to secure remission of sins... the justification of sin without the justification of the sinner. (p. 35)

In contradistinction:

> Costly grace is the treasure hidden in the field; for the sake of it a man will gladly go and sell all that he has. It is the pearl of great price to buy which the merchant will sell all his goods.... Costly grace is the gospel which must be *sought* again and again, the gift

---

[*] Bonhoeffer (1959).

which must be *asked* for, the door at which a man must *knock*.... It is costly because it costs a man his life, and it is grace because it gives a man his own true life." (ibid., pp. 36–37)

This distinction should sound familiar, given our earlier consideration of extrinsic versus intrinsic religiosity. Faith as a love relationship, and as a costly gift is also reminiscent of Pargament's positive versus negative religious coping.

Central to identifying spiritual resources for the individual suffering from existential angst is clarifying whether his faith is authentic, "costly," and intrinsic or superficial, "cheap," and extrinsic.

Guilt

In Chapter 2, we saw that moral concerns can both precipitate and be distorted by depression. Guilt, remorse, and shame stemming either from failures to achieve one's ideals or from behavior that harms others (such as neglect of one's children during periods of substance abuse) can also burden patients in ways that at first glance resemble a mood disorder. Arthur Kleinman[*] highlights the challenge of distinguishing guilt from depression in his book *What Really Matters: Living a Moral Life Amidst Uncertainty and Danger,* for example in his account of a World War II veteran tormented by having killed an unarmed Japanese medic.

---

[*] Kleinman (2006).

Focusing on guilt that may be less conscious, Robert Coles[*] described a case he presented to Anna Freud of a widow who remained angry, difficult, and embittered after years of therapy, presumably for depression. She responded:

> I will confess to you: when I was listening to all of this, I thought to myself that this poor old lady doesn't need us at all. No, she's had her fill of "us," even if she doesn't know it. She's been visiting one or another of "us" for years, decades, as she has dealt with her son's troubles, her husband's, her own. What she needs, I thought, is forgiveness. She needs to make peace with her soul, not talk about her mind. There must be a God, somewhere, to help her, to hear her, to heal her—so I thought for a second! But I fear she'll not find him! (p. 180)

> A 40-year-old teacher and father of two came for treatment after his wife had threatened divorce over his use of pornography. He felt down, disappointed with himself, and frustrated with his inability to deal more effectively with his impulses and his relationship with his wife. Exploration revealed ways that his chronic frustration had fueled escape into sexual fantasy, and that his guilt over this had prevented him from confronting his wife when she became controlling, or critical.

In this case guilt was both as a heavy burden and an obstacle to resolving important interpersonal challenges.

THE "DARK NIGHT OF THE SOUL"

St. John of the Cross, a 16th century Spanish mystic, described the dark night of the soul as an experience of disenchantment

---
[*] Coles (1998).

with a person's usual spirituality. God may seem distant, prayer empty, and meditation forced. The individual may find himself struggling to find gratification elsewhere, questioning God, or becoming confused by his attempts to understand.[*] However, if this obscure (dark) process is marked by a desire to love God, it actually represents growth in that relationship at an unconscious level. St. John distinguished two phases in this process. In the first, the "dark night of the senses," the individual becomes disenchanted with its usual activities—in St. John's image, as a log is blackened by a fire. Emmer[†] summarizes the three indicators of this phase as follows:

1. The soul finds no satisfaction in either the things of God or in other creatures.
2. The soul is troubled by the impression that it has turned away from God; it interprets its distaste for the things of God as a falling away from Him.
3. The soul finds itself no longer capable of meditating and using the imagination in its prayer, despite fervent attempts to do so.

During the second, "dark night of the spirit," the soul is challenged to let go of core, self-centered assumptions and commitments that prevent union with God. In St. John's imagery, the log is not only blackened, but consumed. Eventually, the suffering caused by raw sensitivity to the world leads to the awareness of a path. In St. John's words, "Undetected I slip away—my house, at last, grown still."

---

[*] May (2004).
[†] Emmer (2004).

In the dark night of the soul, an individual loses the ability to enjoy God and life, but unlike in classical depression, still feels a strong desire to know and to please Him. The psychiatrist Gerald May notes that, while the dark night of the soul may be complicated by depression, it is typically not accompanied by a loss of effectiveness, a sense of humor or compassion for others.[*]

> A 50-year-old hospital chaplain came for worsening depression marked by lack of energy, social withdrawal, and diminished interest. During her twenties she had multiple hospitalizations for depression, years of psychotherapy, and trials of several medications. Several factors eventually seemed to help her stabilize for decades before she returned to treatment. These included an antidepressant prescribed by her primary care physician, engaging in meaningful work, becoming a nun (when she said she relinquished her desire for a spouse in favor of intimacy with God), and meeting regularly with a spiritual director. She returned to treatment following a number of losses, when the antidepressant seemed to have lost its effectiveness. After a change in medication and a period of supportive psychotherapy, she described feeling "pretty good" again. A few months later, she entered a painful period of doubt and restlessness, during which she said, "I don't think I'm depressed; I think I'm in a spiritual crisis." One precipitant was a church lecture series on the historical Jesus that made her begin to wonder how much evidence there was for her faith. "Maybe 'the guys' made this up a couple of hundred years later like 'the guys' have made up things in the church all along." Additional precipitants were losing her spiritual director, and seeing the church where she worshipped ordered to close. After meeting with a spiritual director who offered her readings rather than listening to her doubts, she found another who was more helpful, and later

---

[*] May (1982, pp. 84–92).

reported a restored sense of connection with God, as well as a return of her normal mood.

This patient's spiritual crisis, while distinct from her earlier depression, may not fit the classic definition of the "Dark Night." To know, one would need to know more about her experience of God and the realignments that took place as she emerged from this painful period of doubt.

Ordinary Unhappiness

Freud once identified the goal of psychoanalysis as the replacement of neurotic misery with the ordinary unhappiness of life. Yet our therapeutic culture,[*] bolstered by the claims of the pharmaceutical and self-help industries, encourages the belief that happiness is achievable with the use of appropriate technology. Heightened expectations now bring to clinicians' offices more individuals who are unhappy in life than Freud could have foreseen. Critics such as Horwitz and Wakefield[†] argue that our reliance on DSM terminology has "transformed normal sorrow into depressive disorder."

> A 50-year-old small businessman sought treatment several years after surgery for head and neck cancer because of feeling "depressed all my life," though without somatic symptoms of depression. Dyslexia

---

[*] Rieff (1966).
[†] Horwitz and Wakefield (2007).

had contributed to feelings of inferiority, for which he compensated by working hard and driving hard business deals. A divorce, a disappointing second marriage, and a serious motor vehicle accident left him feeling unlucky, cynical, and deprived of what others he saw around him have. He used the therapy hour to recount his various chronic stressors and to ask whether his psychiatrist had "anything better" than the large dose of the antidepressant he was taking.

The positive psychology movement has grown rapidly in recent years.[*] More than 800 Harvard undergraduates now take the course Positive Psychology taught by Tal D. Ben-Shahar. This growth is partly a response to the search for happiness and partly to psychiatry's historical emphasis on pathology rather than on how to live well.

Several themes in positive psychology point to a spiritual dimension of happiness: (1) Positive psychology emphasizes the role of attitude, and of mindfulness in changing it to be more realistic. Failing to acknowledge that life is hard contributes to unnecessary unhappiness. (2) Virtues such as wisdom, courage, and fairness that describe the good life are for many people grounded in an ordered view of the world. (3) Love and forgiveness point beyond the self to larger realities. As a result, evaluating an individual's happiness involves assessing how much his spirituality involves positive emotions, fosters positive traits, and encourages participation in constructive community life.

---

[*] Seligman et al. (2005).

Spiritual Complications of Depression

As we saw in the previous chapter, depression can undermine spirituality. This can reach clinical significance in at least two ways. In the first, a spiritual concern such as a loss of faith can be distressing enough to warrant clinical attention (cf. the V code for Religious or Spiritual Problem, in DSM-IV). In the second, the patient's spiritual interpretation of his depression leads him to resist treatment because he believes that God is trying to teach him something through his suffering, which he deserves and must accept.

Assessment

Patients seeing a mental health professional expect to be asked about depression, but they may be less sure why a clinician is asking about their spirituality. An interviewer who asks general, screening questions such as "Are you a religious or spiritual person?" along with screening questions for depression indicates that he is open to hearing about this sensitive area of life and understands that it could have some importance. Following up in response to positive answers is then a natural way to characterize the type and degree of the patient's spirituality and depression: "How depressed have you been?" "Are you part of a spiritual community?" "Which one?" "Is there someone from your congregation who knows what is going on with you?" "Do you have spiritual practices that are helpful to you?" "Which have been the most helpful?" If the patient's initial answers suggest that spirituality has been a source of distress, the interviewer can then ask for more detail about how this has been the case.

A more in-depth interview regarding spirituality could take several possible directions. From the perspective of what is most therapeutically relevant, it is often helpful for an interviewer to simultaneously follow a two-part strategy: (1) listening to decide on the basis of an initial hypothesis what immediate care will most likely be needed and (2) gathering information needed to formulate a comprehensive treatment plan. Immediate decisions include: (1) whether the individual is suicidal, and if so needs protective intervention; (2) whether the individual should be evaluated for a somatic treatment such as antidepressant medication; and (3) whether psychotherapeutic or spiritual care is likely indicated. The algorithm in Figure 3.1 suggests a sequence for answering these questions.

To develop a focused treatment plan, a clinician will want to assess which conditions are most affecting the individual's functioning. For example, is demoralization, or an adjustment to a loss of faith a significant source of distress?[*] Is depression related to trauma behind the patient's inability to believe?

---

[*] Assessing spiritual functioning, as noted in Chapter 1, involves assessing one's connection to larger reality as engaged vs. static, integrated vs. ambivalent or torn, contemplative or attuned vs. distracted, mature vs. developmentally delayed, and feeling loved vs. rejected by the Other.

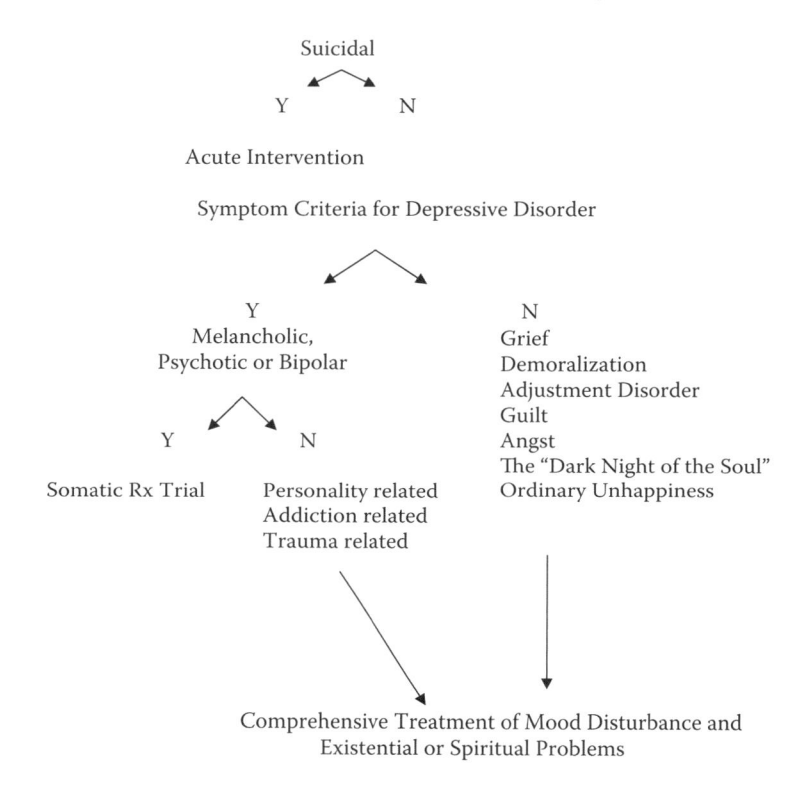

```
                    Suicidal
                    ↙    ↘
                  Y        N
          Acute Intervention

        Symptom Criteria for Depressive Disorder
                    ↙    ↘
          Y                    N
    Melancholic,             Grief
  Psychotic or Bipolar       Demoralization
        ↙    ↘               Adjustment Disorder
      Y        N             Guilt
                             Angst
  Somatic Rx Trial   Personality related    The "Dark Night of the Soul"
                     Addiction related      Ordinary Unhappiness
                     Trauma related
                              ↘                ↓
            Comprehensive Treatment of Mood Disturbance and
                    Existential or Spiritual Problems
```

Figure 3.1 Algorithm for making initial treatment decisions in patients with depressed mood and spiritual concerns.

A clinician's own spirituality can influence his perspective on this key question. For example, a clinician whose larger reality is empiricism may reduce spiritual functioning to psychological processes and focus his attention there. Conversely, a clinician convinced of the reality of a supernatural realm may see the patient's emotional struggles as less important than the choices he makes in responding to God.

A full assessment involves answering further questions: What is the patient's primary concern? Is it relief of symptoms? A more coherent understanding of his situation? A closer relationship to others, including God? If a primary goal of the patient is spiritual health, do his conceptions of spiritual and mental health coincide? Put another way, is his goal to more fully address existential issues of hope, identity, connection, and meaning/purpose? Or do his spiritual and emotional goals conflict, in areas such as embracing suffering vs. avoiding pain, obeying God vs. self-actualizing, thinking in terms of this life vs. the next, or sacrificing one's own interests vs. pursuing enlightened self-interest? A patient might appropriately fear mental health treatment that does not take these goals into account.

What is the major existential task facing the patient at this point in his life? Is it, in Eriksonian terms, developing basic trust, autonomy, initiative, integrity? Is the patient mastering or overwhelmed by this task?

How do the patient's and therapist's spiritual beliefs shape their priorities? A religious patient may refuse needed medication for depression because she feels she should instead pray for more faith. Her psychiatrist might wish to challenge her belief because of the priority he places on using established means for treating depression. However, if he regards her world view as pathological and escapist without being aware of how his own world view is influencing his approach to her, the treatment is likely to be unempathic and unnecessarily confrontational. Conversely, if a therapist is unaware that his religious identification with a depressed trauma survivor causes him to focus more on her spiritual concerns than on her depression, he may neglect her need for medication.

Finally, what are the resistances of the patient to accepting treatment? Are diminished energy, hopelessness, helplessness, worthlessness, or guilt blocking effective participation? Do these have spiritual components? For example, does a patient feel unworthy of treatment because he feels that God is punishing him? Or, does he have spiritual objections to particular treatment modalities? For example, some individuals fear that medication will distract them from, or numb them to the reasons for their depression. Others are concerned that medication will be soul numbing because it discourages them from relying only on God for help. Still others believe that psychotherapy, unless it applies scriptural principles directly to one's life, undermines faith.

Formulation

Clinical assessment ideally culminates in the construction of an empirically grounded, comprehensive case formulation that (1) organizes the key facts of case around a centrally important causal/explanatory source, (2) frames this source in terms of factors amenable to direct intervention, and (3) anticipates the potential role of both risk and protective factors in the treatment (In a psychodynamic formulation, these would include how the patient's central conflict is likely to play out in resistance, transference, and countertransference). Traditional, multiaxial diagnostic formulations attempt to characterize various dimensions of the patient's difficulties using standardized criteria. Recognizing the importance of contextualizing these in relation to genetic and constitutional factors, psychological processes such as motivation, ego functioning, and sociocultural factors, Faulkner et al. (1985) have called for flexibility in individualizing the clinician's understanding of the case. One step in this direction was the inclusion of an Outline for a Cultural Formulation in DSM-IV. One of its authors[*] has since proposed ways that the Outline for DSM-V could be revised to include religious and spiritual factors.

In practical terms, to integrate information about the depressed patient's existential concerns and spiritual life into the formulation of the case, it may help to ask the following questions: What are the patient's vulnerabilities to depressed mood? What is the relationship among these factors? Why has the individual become symptomatic now? What is causing him the most impairment or distress? What resources are available for addressing his current state and underlying vulnerabilities? And what are the obstacles to drawing on these resources?

What are the patient's vulnerabilities to depression? Is there a biological diathesis (melancholic, psychotic, bipolar, or personality-based depression), an unresolved legacy of trauma,

---

[*] Gellerman and Lu (2011).

disappointment related to unrealistic expectations (demoralization, adjustment disorder, ordinary unhappiness), a set of consequences stemming from addiction-related or other behavior (addiction, guilt), or an impasse in dealing with life (choice in the case of angst, loss in the case of grief, or the dark night of the soul in the case of a relationship to God)?

What is the relationship among these vulnerabilities? Which seem to be primary and which secondary? A patient may present suicidal and preoccupied by guilt that is related to addiction behavior. He may be devastated after the loss of a relationship because he lacks basic trust due to early trauma, because he has expected that person to provide unconditional love, or to make up for the loss of an inadequate parent. Or his relationship to God may suffer from the same kind of fear and avoidance that mark his relationship with other potential sources of help.

Why has the individual become symptomatic now? Is the presenting episode representative of a pattern, for example of seasonal depression, of despair after a particular kind of loss, or of expecting too much from another poorly chosen partner? The personal meaning of the precipitating stressor determines its significance. An inability to read may be devastating to a patient who has valued his mind, but not to one who does not.

What is impairing or distressing him most? Whereas mild discouragement can be a useful incentive to reassess one's priorities and to change direction, disabling depression requires prompt intervention, whatever its cause.

What resources are available for addressing the patient's current state and underlying vulnerabilities? These might be biological (e.g., medication), psychological (e.g., insight, adaptive defenses such as humor), social (e.g., the care and input of family, friends, and professionals), or spiritual (practices, beliefs, and experiences that serve to connect one with a larger reality). Does the religious bipolar patient have a pastor who can support medication, or ECT? Has music, or time spent with nature been a way for the patient adjusting to cancer to feel grounded? What rituals can help a patient to grieve, or to deal with grief? Are there beliefs that can help a demoralized individual regain his balance and sense of hope? What has brought a person through previous "dark nights of the soul?" What has the trauma survivor learned about himself and the world from previous periods of suffering? How does an unhappy person want to be able to respond to adversity? Are there ways such as mindfulness he can use for dealing with unrealistic desires? Have Twelve Step programs been helpful to the depressed addict, and in what way? Has a relationship with God or a spiritual community been sustaining to the patient with a personality disorder? In what way?

Implied in this question is the task of matching the available resources to the most pressing symptoms and most important vulnerabilities. Is a pastor the most appropriate resource for a patient distressed over his loss of faith, or is a psychological resource such as therapy for a traumatic past? The answer may depend on the next question.

What are the obstacles to drawing on these resources? Do melancholic symptoms make it too difficult for a patient to concentrate on insight oriented, or cognitive psychotherapy? Does childhood abuse by a pastor make it difficult to refer a patient to the spiritual resources of his church? Is a religious patient too mistrustful of secular psychiatry to accept referral to a therapist who does not share his world view? Does the person struggling with guilt assume that God could not forgive him because of what he learned in Sunday School? Does he have intellectual reservations about accepting the possibility of both supernatural intervention and science? Is he accustomed to compartmentalizing his religious and secular life so that one does not influence the other? Is he angry with God for a painful loss? Has he been disillusioned by seeing an admired mentor stumble, or betray his ideals?

In summary, we have emphasized here the traditional importance of a differential diagnosis and comprehensive formulation as a basis for the clinician's approach. For example, identifying depressive symptoms as melancholic or not can suggest whether a trial of somatic therapy is indicated. And assessment of suicide risk and degree of distress determines whether an issue requires urgent intervention. We have seen further how differentiating among types of disorder marked by low mood can help clinicians recognize which vulnerabilities (such as addiction, trauma, or loss) and their spiritual complications are most clinically relevant. Understanding the patients' goals, resources, and obstacles to drawing upon these are all important in shaping the clinical formulation of the problems that the depressed individual has in living well—due both to distressing symptoms and to the underlying vulnerabilities in his heart, mind, and soul. In the next chapter we explore the challenges of taking these on in the role of a clinician.

By way of illustration, consider the following sample initial formulation:

> This 33-year-old underemployed Protestant salesman presents with guilt over compulsive use of Internet pornography, and a recurrence of mild depression since breaking up with his girlfriend, both of which seem particularly painful because they remind him of his father's failed relationships with women. Despite no family history of depression, his past response to an antidepressant suggests that he may benefit again from medication if psychotherapy directed at his identification with his father and related concerns is ineffective. A recent, more positive view of how God sees him that has resulted from involvement in a church-related men's group indicates that his faith may be an important resource. However, his past inconsistent use of all of these resources means that his ambivalence about receiving help will need to be promptly explored and addressed directly.

References

Akiskal, H.S., & McKinney, W.T., Jr. (1973). Depressive disorders: Toward a unified hypothesis. *Science,* 182, 20–29.

Balboni, T.A., Vanderwerker, L.C., Block, S.D., Paulk, M.E., Lathan, C.S., Peteet, J.R. et al. (2007). Religiousness and spiritual support among advanced cancer patients and associations with end-of-life treatment preferences and quality of life. *J Clin Oncol, 25,* 555–560.

Biro, M., & Till, E. (1989). Factor analytic study of depressive disorders. *J Clin Psychol,* 45, 369–373.

Blazer, D.G. (2005). *The Age of Melancholy: "Major Depression" and Its Social Origins.* New York: Routledge.

Block, S.D. (2001). Psychological considerations, growth, and transcendence at the end of life: The art of the possible. *JAMA,* 285, 2898–2905.

Bonhoeffer, D. (1959). *The Cost of Discipleship* (2nd ed.). New York: Macmillan.

Borg, J., Andree, B., Soderstrom, H., & Farde, L. (2003). The serotonin system and spiritual experiences. *Am J Psychiatry,* 160, 1965–1969.

Breslau, N., Peterson, E.L., Schultz, L.R., Chilcoat, H.D., & Andreski, P. (1998). Major depression and stages of smoking. A longitudinal investigation. *Arch Gen Psychiatry,* 55, 161–166.

Campbell, J.C., Kub, J., Belknap, R.A., & Templin, T.N. (1997). Predictors of depression in battered women. *Violence Against Women,* 3, 271–293.

Cassell, E.J. (1992). The nature of suffering: Physical, psychological, social, and spiritual aspects. *NLN Publ* (15-2461), 1–10.

Charney, D.S., Nelson, J.C., & Quinlan, D.M. (1981). Personality traits and disorder in depression. *Am J Psychiatry,* 138, 1601–1604.

Clarke, D.M., & Kissane, D.W. (2002). Demoralization: Its phenomenology and importance. *Aust N Z J Psychiatry,* 36, 733–742.

Clayton, P.J., Halikas, J.A., & Maurice, W.L. (1972). The depression of widowhood. *Br J Psychiatry,* 120, 71–77.

Cloninger, C.R. (2006). The science of well being: An integrated approach to mental health and its disorders. *Psychiatr Danub,* 18, 218–224.

Cloninger, C.R., Svrakic, D.M., & Przybeck, T.R. (1993). A psychobiological model of temperament and character. *Arch Gen Psychiatry,* 50, 975–990.

Coles, R. (1988). *Harvard Diary: Reflections on the Sacred and the Secular.* New York: Crossroad.

Corruble, E., Ginestet, D., & Guelfi, J.D. (1996). Comorbidity of personality disorders and unipolar major depression: A review. *J Affect Disord,* 37, 157–170.

Coyne, J.C., & Whiffen, V.E. (1995). Issues in personality as diathesis for depression: The case of sociotropy-dependency and autonomy-self-criticism. *Psychol Bull,* 118, 358–378.

Emmer, C. (2004). Discernment of the dark night of the senses. The Weight of Glory, March 24, 2004. http://www.doxaweb.com/blog/2004/03/discernment-of-night-of-senses.htm.   Accessed September 21, 2008.

Faulkner, L.R., Kinzie, J.D., & Angell, R. (1985). A comprehensive psychiatric formulation model. *J Psychiatric Ed,* 9, 189–203.

Fava, M., Alpert, J.E., Borus, J.S., Nierenberg, A.A., Pava, J.A., & Rosenbaum, J.F. (1996). Patterns of personality disorder comorbidity in early-onset versus late-onset major depression. *Am J Psychiatry,* 153, 1308–1312.

Fava, M., Bouffides, E., Pava, J.A., McCarthy, M.K., Steingard, R.J., & Rosenbaum, J.F. (1994). Personality disorder comorbidity with major depression and response to fluoxetine treatment. *Psychother Psychosom,* 62, 160–167.

Gellerman, D.M., & Lu, F.G. (2011). Religious and spiritual issues in the Outline for Cultural Formulation. In J.R. Peteet, W. Narrow, & F.G. Lu (Eds.), *Religious and Spiritual Issues in Psychiatric Diagnosis: A Research Agenda for DSM-V.* Washington, DC: American Psychiatric Publishing, Inc.

Griffith, J.L., & Gaby, L. (2005). Brief psychotherapy at the bedside: Countering demoralization from medical illness. *Psychosomatics,* 46, 109–116.

Herman, J.L. (1992). *Trauma and Recovery.* New York: Basic Books.

Horwitz, A.V., & Wakefield, J.C. (2007). *The Loss of Sadness: How Psychiatry Transformed Normal Sorrow into Depressive Disorder.* New York: Oxford University Press.

Horowitz, M.J., Siegel, B., Holen, A., Bonanno, G.A., Milbrath, C., & Stinson, C.H. (2003). Diagnostic criteria for complicated grief disorder. *Focus,* 1, 290–298.

Hutto, B. (2001). Potential overdiagnosis of bipolar disorder. *Psychiatr Serv,* 52, 687–688.

Kendler, K.S., Gardner, C.O., & Prescott, C.A. (2006). Toward a comprehensive developmental model for major depression in men. *Am J Psychiatry,* 163, 115–124.

Kendler, K.S., Kessler, R.C., Neale, M.C., Heath, A.C., & Eaves, L.J. (1993). The prediction of major depression in women: Toward an integrated etiologic model. *Am J Psychiatry,* 150, 1139–1148.

Kierkegaard, S. (1954). *Fear and Trembling, and The Sickness Unto Death.* Garden City, NY: Doubleday.

Kleinman, A. (2006). *What Really Matters: Living a Moral Life Amidst Uncertainty and Danger.* New York: Oxford University Press.

Kramer, P.D. (1997). *Listening to Prozac.* New York: Penguin Books.

Mangelli, L., Fava, G.A., Grandi, S., Grassi, L., Ottolini, F., Porcelli, P. et al. (2005). Assessing demoralization and depression in the setting of medical disease. *J Clin Psychiatry,* 66, 391–394.

Marcos, T., & Salamero, M. (1990). Factor study of the Hamilton Rating Scale for Depression and the Bech Melancholia Scale. *Acta Psychiatr Scand,* 82, 178–181.

May, R. (1969). *Existential Psychology* (2nd ed.). New York: Random House.

May, G.G. (1982). *Care of Mind, Care of Spirit: Psychiatric Dimensions of Spiritual Direction* (1st ed.). San Francisco: Harper & Row.

May, G.G. (2004). *The Dark Night of the Soul: A Psychiatrist Explores the Connection Between Darkness and Spiritual Growth.* New York: HarperCollins Publishers, Inc.

Mollica, R.F., McInnes, K., Poole, C., & Tor, S. (1998). Dose-effect relationships of trauma to symptoms of depression and post-traumatic stress disorder among Cambodian survivors of mass violence. *Br J Psychiatry,* 173, 482–488.

Momartin, S., Silove, D., Manicavasagar, V., & Steel, Z. (2004). Comorbidity of PTSD and depression: Associations with trauma exposure, symptom severity and functional impairment in Bosnian refugees resettled in Australia. *J Affect Disord,* 80, 231–238.

Neimeyer, R.A., Prigerson, H.G., & Davis, B. (2002). Mourning and meaning. *American Behavioral Scientist,* 46, 235–251.

Norris, K. (2008). *Acedia and Me: A Marriage, Monks and a Writer's Life.* New York: Riverhead Books.

Nunes, E.V., & Levin, F.R. (2004). Treatment of depression in patients with alcohol or other drug dependence: A meta-analysis. *JAMA*, 291, 1887–1896.

O'Donnell, M.L., Creamer, M., & Pattison, P. (2004). Posttraumatic stress disorder and depression following trauma: Understanding comorbidity. *Am J Psychiatry*, 161, 1390–1396.

Parker, G. (2000). Classifying depression: Should paradigms lost be regained? *Am J Psychiatry*, 157, 1195–1203.

Peteet, J.R. (1985). Religious issues presented by cancer patients seen in psychiatric consultation. *J Psychosocial Oncology*, 3, 53–66.

Peteet, J.R. (1993). A closer look at the role of a spiritual approach in addictions treatment. *J Subst Abuse Treat*, 10, 263–267.

Peteet, J.R. (2001). Putting suffering into perspective: Implications of the patient's world view. *J Psychother Pract Res,* 10, 187–192.

Phillips, K.A., Gunderson, J.G., Hirschfeld, R.M., & Smith, L.E. (1990). A review of the depressive personality. *Am J Psychiatry*, 147, 830–837.

Phillips, K.A., Gunderson, J.G., Triebwasser, J., Kimble, C.R., Faedda, G., Lyoo, I.K. et al. (1998). Reliability and validity of depressive personality disorder. *Am J Psychiatry*, 155, 1044–1048.

Prigerson, H.G., Frank, E., Kasl, S.V., Reynolds, C.F., 3rd, Anderson, B., Zubenko, G.S. et al. (1995). Complicated grief and bereavement-related depression as distinct disorders: Preliminary empirical validation in elderly bereaved spouses. *Am J Psychiatry*, 152, 22–30.

Regier, D.A., Farmer, M.E., Rae, D.S., Locke, B.Z., Keith, S.J., Judd, L.L. et al. (1990). Comorbidity of mental disorders with alcohol and other drug abuse. Results from the Epidemiologic Catchment Area (ECA) Study. *JAMA,* 264, 2511–2518.

Rieff, P. (1966). *The Triumph of the Therapeutic: Uses of Faith After Freud* (1st ed.). New York: Harper & Row.

Sanderson, W.C., Wetzler, S., Beck, A.T., & Betz, F. (1992). Prevalence of personality disorders in patients with major depression and dysthymia. *Psychiatry Res,* 42, 93–99.

Schatzberg, A.F. (2006). New paradigm for treating recurrent depression: From symptom control to managing enduring vulnerabilities. *CNS Spectr,* 11(12 Suppl 15), 22–27.

Schuckit, M.A. (2006). Comorbidity between substance use disorders and psychiatric conditions. *Addiction, 101 Suppl* 1, 76–88.

Seligman, M.E., Steen, T.A., Park, N., & Peterson, C. (2005). Positive psychology progress: Empirical validation of interventions. *Am Psychol,* 60, 410–421.

Senter, K., & Caldwell, K. (2002). Spirituality and the maintenance of change: A phenomenological study of women who leave abusive relationships. *J Contemporary Family Therapy,* 24, 543–564.

Shalev, A.Y., Freedman, S., Peri, T., Brandes, D., Sahar, T., Orr, S.P. et al. (1998). Prospective study of posttraumatic stress disorder and depression following trauma. *Am J Psychiatry,* 155, 630–637.

Shea, M.T., Pilkonis, P.A., Beckham, E., Collins, J.F., Elkin, I., Sotsky, S.M. et al. (1990). Personality disorders and treatment outcome in the NIMH Treatment of Depression Collaborative Research Program. *Am J Psychiatry,* 147, 711–718.

Slavney, P.R. (1999). Diagnosing demoralization in consultation psychiatry. *Psychosomatics,* 40, 325–329.

Solomon, A. (2001). *The Noonday Demon: An Atlas of Depression.* New York: Scribner.

Styron, W. (1990). *Darkness Visible: A Memoir of Madness.* New York: Random House.

Sulmasy, D.P. (2006). Spiritual issues in the care of dying patients: "... it's okay between me and God." *JAMA,* 296, 1385–1392.

Tillich, P. (1952). *The Courage to Be.* New Haven: Yale University Press.

Viederman, M., & Perry, S.W., 3rd. (1980). Use of a psychodynamic life narrative in the treatment of depression in the physically ill. *Gen Hosp Psychiatry,* 2, 177–185.

Wakefield, J.C., Schmitz, M.F., First, M.B., & Horwitz, A.V. (2007). Extending the bereavement exclusion for major depression to other losses: Evidence from the National Comorbidity Survey. *Arch Gen Psychiatry,* 64, 433–440.

Yalom, I.D. (1980). *Existential Psychotherapy.* New York: Basic Books.

4 Integrated Treatment

> Thinking well is wise; planning well, wiser; but doing well is the wisest and best of all.
>
> **Persian Proverb**

Are spiritual approaches helpful in depression, and if so, how? Although clinicians are understandably skeptical of claims by spiritual practitioners to cure depression, there is growing evidence that spiritually oriented approaches can play a significant role in its treatment. In this chapter I review these, suggest a framework for using them, and discuss practical aspects of incorporating them into clinical practice.

Spiritual Approaches

Religiously oriented cognitive behavior therapy (CBT), the best studied of these approaches, draws on an individual's own tradition to teach and modify cognitions in the service of change.[*] Key interventions include disputation using scriptural or other

---
[*] Hodge (2006).

religious evidence to combat irrational or self-defeating beliefs that are inconsistent with the patient's faith; religious imagery for comfort, or to reduce anxiety; and prayer or scripture reading as adjunctive cognitive homework.[*] The focus of CBT on core beliefs as essential elements of feeling and behavior makes it particularly congruent with Christianity, Judaism, Buddhism, and Islam.[†] Tan and Johnson[‡] have reviewed six studies of Christian CBT and two of Muslim CBT in reducing depression, as well as others in treating anxiety. In one of the best known, Probst et al.[§] compared the efficacy of religious CBT (using religiously oriented challenges to cognitive distortions) and nonreligious CBT in a group of 59 Christian patients with mild depression who considered religious or spiritual issues important or very important. After 18 to 20 one-hour sessions over three months, patients who received religiously based treatment reported significantly less posttreatment depression. Interestingly, religiously oriented treatment delivered by nonreligious therapists was as effective as that delivered by religious therapists.

A second approach is mindfulness-based cognitive therapy (MBCT). With roots in the Buddhist tradition, MBCT posits a model of cognitive vulnerability to depressive relapse

---

[*] Tan et al. (2005, p. 81).
[†] Nielsen et al. (2001).
[‡] Tan and Johnson (2005).
[§] Probst et al. (1992).

advanced by Segal[*] and others. This model assumes that recovered depressed patients differ from never-depressed individuals in that their episodes of mild depression activate patterns of negative thinking similar to those that were dominant during periods of major depression. MBCT aims to help patients become more aware of these patterns and more able to disengage from them. The central idea is that moment-by-moment, nonjudgmental awareness fosters a "decentered" perspective on thoughts and feelings. But Segal goes further:

> If we are to make changes at this deeper level, we need to do more than provide patients with new conceptual information about depression, negative thinking, and relapse. Instead, we need to provide new experiences for the mind and body, over and over again, that will accumulate to create an alternative view. (p. 67)

Ma et al.[†] confirmed earlier findings of Teasdale et al.[‡] that MBCT was effective in reducing relapse to a rate of 36 percent as compared to 78 percent in a cohort of 55 patients with three previous depressive episodes.

Meditation, which is an important means of achieving mindfulness, has other emotional and physical benefits, such as the elicitation of the relaxation response. The availability of generic forms of meditation has made it acceptable to recommend within secular mental health settings. However, Wachholtz et al.[§] found

---

[*] Segal et al. (2002).
[†] Ma and Teasdale (2004).
[‡] Teasdale and Johnson (2000).
[§] Wachholtz and Pargament (2005).

that subjects who practiced spiritual meditation showed more positive mood and greater pain tolerance than those who practiced secular meditation or relaxation techniques. They suggest that secular forms of meditation are *less*-spiritually oriented, rather than *non*-spiritually oriented.

A third approach centers on helping suffering individuals find meaning and exercise choice. Folkman and Greer[*] describe ways that a therapist can explore meaning and purpose, and help individuals identify realistic and meaningful goals whatever their situation may be. Following the principles of Victor Frankl's[†] logotherapy, they encourage patients to look for meaning in valued experiences, creative action, and virtues such as compassion, bravery, or humor. Breitbart[‡] incorporates these principles into meaning-centered group psychotherapy for patients with advanced cancer. Twelve Step Programs such as Alcoholics Anonymous also encourage members to pursue choices in relation to a Higher Power (over addiction proneness, character defects, or "wreckage from the past").

A fourth group of approaches—humanistic psychotherapy, forgiveness-promoting therapy, and positive psychology—deals with the value concerns of depressed individuals.

Humanistic psychologists since Maslow have emphasized the universal importance of spiritual values such as wonder,

---

[*] Folkman and Greer (2000).

[†] Frankl (1970).

[‡] Breitbart (2002).

compassion, and gratitude. Elkins[*] describes how he used an exercise to evoke greater awareness of "soul-nourishing" activities in the treatment of a depressed, divorced woman disillusioned by the faith of her childhood.

Over the past three decades, Worthington[†] and others have developed interventions designed to promote forgiveness and reconciliation, and there is a growing literature on their effectiveness for depression. For example, Levenson et al.[‡] reported marked improvement in depressive symptoms in a sample of 99 participants in an emotional educational program that focused on the intergenerational transmission of negative interaction patterns by increasing forgiveness and spirituality, as compared with a group of 47 waiting list controls. Dynamically and supportively oriented therapists are familiar with helping individuals feel accepted so that they are more able to accept themselves and/or receive forgiveness offered by God.

The recent ascendancy of positive psychology has led clinicians to recognize how other virtues such as self-control, love, hope, humility, patience, wisdom, courage, and gratitude can foster resilience, buffering against stressful life events and the development of psychopathology.[§] For example, Seligman et al.[¶]

---

[*] Elkins (2005).

[†] Worthington et al. (2005).

[‡] Levensen et al. (2006).

[§] Peterson and Seligman (2004).

[¶] Seligman et al. (2005).

in a random-assignment, placebo-controlled Internet study found a lasting reduction in depressive symptoms in individuals who practiced three exercises that asked them to focus on using signature strengths in a new way, three good things, and gratitude.

A fifth set of approaches—psychoanalytic psychotherapy, interpersonal therapy (IPT), and spiritual direction—works with spiritual relationships as important psychic realities in treatment. Owing to the work of object relations theorists such as Ana-Maria Rizzuto,[*] analysts have come to appreciate the potential for the analytic situation to provide "a unique psychological space through which religious associations, spiritual experiences, and God-representations may be elicited and through with the origins and psychodynamic functions of personal religious ideas may be disclosed."[†] Shafranske describes the successful analytic treatment of an anxious lawyer who worked through her feelings about her volatile father and her scattered mother that were reflected in her conflicted relationship to God and the church. Late in the treatment, after the death of a friend, she reported "feeling in ever-increasing moments that life was a wonderful opportunity and that she was cared for in some everlasting way. She reported that her sense of the presence of God was different in some essential way—God wasn't really the 'gods' of her childhood any longer, and she felt no anxiety or awe, but rather that

---

[*] Rizzuto (1979).

[†] Shafranske (2005, p. 120).

whatever the divine was, she was accepted." Giving birth to a child led her on a search for a faith community, and the analytic situation continued to provide a place where she could clarify her religious and spiritual beliefs, in light of psychological factors influencing her perspective. Her changing representations of God and relationship to him were important factors in her progressively improving mood, and maturity. It is easy to appreciate how such an anxiously depressed individual could feel better if she were confident that God was in control, was with her, and had her best interests at heart.

Interpersonal therapy (IPT) is a more recent, structured treatment developed by Klerman et al.[*] for moderate and severe depression. It assumes, because the need for relationships is central and because depression occurs in a social context, that helping individuals to renegotiate the social context can help lift the symptoms of depression, improve social functioning, and protect against future episodes. Spiritually oriented IPT addresses transitions, conflicts, grief, and interpersonal deficits within the context of one's relationships with God, spiritual authorities, or fellow believers. An example might be psychotherapy focused on understanding and taking action to address a depressed patient's loss of faith after feeling betrayed by a pastor. Are there things the patient could do to clarify the actual situation? To repair the relationship? To identify and resolve its impact on his accustomed

---

[*] Klerman (1984).

ability to trust God? In her account of the effective use of spiritually oriented IPT to prevent depression in a group of pregnant adolescents in Harlem, Lisa Miller[*] describes helping them to experience their role as mothers within a spiritual context.

In the ancient process of spiritual direction, a guide or director accompanies an individual searching for spiritual growth as he explores his awareness of and response to the divine.[†] Spiritual direction assumes that the most basic human longing is for transcendent connectedness and surrender, but also that this longing is ambivalent. Sperry[‡] has concisely compared psychotherapy and spiritual direction: The spiritual director listens for spiritual meaning in ways that foster wholeness, healing, and transformation rather than for pathology with a view to cure. Transformation that reflects healing, rather than character change or symptom relief, is "the process of undergoing a radical change of mind and heart, a dying to the false self and a continually assenting to one's true self that reflects the image and likeness of God." The focus is therefore on the individual's relationship to God rather than on his relationship to the therapist, or to others. Prayer, meditation, and spiritual practices such as Ignatian exercises may be important means of deepening this relationship. Although an individual would not ordinarily engage a spiritual director to treat his depression, clinicians who are expert in both psychotherapy

---

[*] Miller (2005).

[†] Benner (2005).

[‡] Sperry (2005, p. 310).

and direction have described incorporating spiritual direction into their care. For example, Benner[*] has described treating a depressed lesbian woman with a history of abusive relationships with men who experienced considerable emotional healing and improvement in her mood as their use of imaginative exercises helped her to feel God's love for her. Another example is Sperry's[†] treatment of a depressed and perfectionistic woman whom he encouraged in her use of centering prayer, meditation, a retreat, and participation in a healthy religious community. Discussion of her spiritual life in relation to other domains allowed her to become more at peace with herself and to taper off of antidepressant medication. Spiritual direction can also be a means of addressing depressive guilt, when the therapist asks the individual whose voice he is listening to—the Accuser's, or God's?

> An office worker who has struggled with depression for years and had been very hesitant to leave her dreary job to find one in the arts finally experienced a breakthrough when she felt God was telling her that He wanted her to play. Rather than fearing that she was doing the wrong thing, or becoming compulsive about learning new Media Art skills, she was now able to enjoy them with a sense of God's blessing on her "play." This helped her to look for work in a new field.

Finally, several approaches integrate various spiritual interventions. Sperry's "integrative" therapy incorporates virtue- and

---

[*] Benner (2005).

[†] Sperry (2005).

strength-based elements of positive psychology with spiritual direction. Benner's[*] "intensive soul care" includes both an existential and a psychodynamic perspective. Richards'[†] "theistic integrative therapy" advocates the use of spiritual along with behavioral, psychodynamic, cognitive, humanistic, and other interventions. Cole and Pargament's[‡] "spiritual/psychotherapeutic intervention for people diagnosed with cancer" combines a focus on existential concerns with one on finding spiritual resources for dealing with them. The supportive-affective group program of Miller et al.[§] addresses the spiritual, emotional, and existential concerns of patients with life-threatening illness. And Twelve Step approaches such as Alcoholics Anonymous (AA) address the concerns of addicted individuals in the areas of identity, an inner life, integrity, and interrelatedness.[¶]

Integrative approaches recognize both that a spiritual problem with existential and psychological roots can contribute to depression, and that enhancing spirituality can contribute directly to its improvement. Consider the example of a religious college student who becomes depressed and disappointed with himself after repeatedly pulling away from his campus ministry to party with his friends. An integrated approach might explore

---

[*] Benner (2005).

[†] Richards (2005).

[‡] Cole and Pargament (1999).

[§] Miller et al. (2005).

[¶] Peteet (1993).

his ambivalence and his inability to sustain his commitments, as well as ways he could clarify and realistically live out his vision, for example by being accountable to a peer.

Integrating Spiritual Approaches

How can a clinician select among these spiritually oriented approaches in treating depression? I suggested in Chapter 2 that depressive conditions, regardless of etiology (Chapter 3), may cause suffering in areas of existential concern such as guilt, meaninglessness, and isolation. The framework in Table 4.1 matches

Table 4.1 Relationship of Spiritually Oriented Interventions to Depressive Concerns

Existential Domain	Depressive Concern	Healthy Spiritual Characteristic	Spiritually Oriented Approach
Identity	Doubt, Disorientation	Engaged, Transformative	Humanistic, Spiritual Direction
Hope	Despair, Mistrust	Integrated	Psychodynamic, CBT, Spiritual Direction, IPT
Meaning / Purpose	Meaninglessness	Attuned, Contemplative	Meaning Centered, Mindfulness, Meditation
Morality	Guilt	Mature	Forgiveness Promoting, Positive Psychology
Authority / Autonomy	Isolation, Rejection	Accepted, Loved	Psychodynamic, IPT, Spiritual Direction

depressed patients' existential concerns with spiritually oriented interventions directed toward helping them acquire the healthy spiritual characteristics described in Chapter 1.

As suggested by the framework suggested in Table 4.1, patients whose existential concerns center around identity, and who are therefore vulnerable to experiencing doubt or disorientation when depressed, may benefit from a more engaged, transformative spirituality that helps them better appreciate who they are. To accomplish this, they may find helpful a humanistic emphasis on connecting with what most fulfills and best defines them. If religious, they may also benefit from grounding their identity in their relationship to God, for example through a process of spiritual direction.

Patients with difficulty maintaining ultimate hope because their experience of the world is fragmented, and who are mistrustful when in despair, would be expected to benefit from achieving a more integrated spirituality. Ways to do so include exploration of unresolved trauma, CBT that brings their core beliefs more in line with their experience, and interpersonal therapy or spiritual direction that focuses on their doubts about trusting God or the future.

Depressed patients who struggle to find a sense of meaning, or who feel their life has lost its purpose, would be expected to benefit from a more attuned, contemplative spirituality. Potential means of realizing this include meaning-centered therapy, mindfulness, and meditation.

Patients concerned with moral questions, such as those who feel overwhelmed by guilt when depressed, would be expected to benefit from a more mature, or age-appropriate spirituality. Therapeutic approaches directed toward this include forgiveness-promoting therapy and the emphasis of positive psychology on virtues such as love.

Patients whose existential concerns center on their relationship to ultimate authority, and who feel isolated or rejected when depressed, would be expected to benefit from feeling accepted and loved by God. Potential therapeutic means to this end include psychodynamically oriented treatment focused on their distorted object relations, interpersonal therapy focused on their relationship to God, and/or spiritual direction.

Spiritually oriented approaches that address concerns in one of these domains—for example, one's relationship to God—may of course also address concerns in other areas, such as identity or hope. For example, the individual who feels loved by God, worshipful, and continually surrendered to his will may be less prone to worship lesser gods such as power or pleasure that will disappoint and leave him depressed.

Practical Aspects of Integration

How does this suggested framework for applying spiritual approaches map onto the range of vulnerabilities to depressed mood that we identified in Chapter 3? It seems clear that a patient struggling with guilt might benefit from a forgiveness-promoting intervention, and one with the dark night of the soul from spiritual direction. But a patient with demoralization or complex grief could have a number of depressive concerns such as meaninglessness, despair, and feelings of isolation or rejection. Such patients, who have more complex clinical pictures, present a number of practical questions: Which aspect of their condition should have priority, and which receive a spiritually oriented approach? What are appropriate goals of spiritual care? What are possible roles of a clinician in pursuing these goals? What is the importance of the patient's and the clinician's world view? What boundaries are important to maintain in dealing with religious and spiritual issues (for example, regarding disclosure of the therapist's own world view)? What common pitfalls need to be avoided?

DECIDING PRIORITIES AND APPROACHES

Arguably, a clinician's first priority is safety, the second is relieving suffering, and the third is improving functioning. The depressive concerns most related to safety are hopelessness and guilt (see the next chapter for a discussion of the spiritual aspects of suicide). In addition to guilt, concerns related to suffering include isolation, rejection, and meaninglessness. Doubt and disorientation directly impair functioning. As a result, different spiritual approaches are likely to be needed at different points in an individual's treatment, as one concern gives way to another.

Adding to the complexity involved in organizing and integrating approaches is the fact that deeper reasons for the patient's suffering often emerge over the course of several sessions—for example, a conscious concern with physical symptoms or recurrent worries may make clear the presence of substance use, painful memories of abuse, or unacknowledged grief. A major challenge for the clinician in deciding priorities is to listen for, and effectively address the conflicts, and their spiritual aspects, that are blocking progress. Consider how some unresolved core conflicts underlie depressive vulnerability when they center around trauma, perfectionism, negative self-identity, or self-sacrifice:

Trauma

Survivors of trauma often suffer from shame, self-imposed isolation, and splitting off of painful memories and aspects of the self. They may feel hopeless, even suicidal, without a coherent sense of themselves in the world. When this hopelessness blocks the patient's attempts to do painful exploratory work, or engage with others, it necessarily takes center stage in the treatment. Spiritual approaches to fostering integration as a basis for hope might, for example, help a patient apply his belief in God's goodness to his current distressed state. When hopeful enough to continue looking at his past, a survivor might then present guilt (for example over neglecting her own children) that is reinforced by memories of verbal abuse, and subsequent self-accusation. Attempts to deal with this by exploring options for forgiveness could then lead to doubts about identity as damaged, defective, or cursed. At this point, approaches that help the patient become more engaged with a larger reality (one who can love and accept her as she realistically is) are relevant, and may be transformative.

> A 60-year-old divorced mother of four presented for treatment of chronic, recently worsened depression after being hospitalized for an overdose that followed an argument with her son. She reported childhood physical and verbal abuse from her working class immigrant parents, who belittled her efforts to cross over to the "other side of the tracks" by pursuing an education. However, teachers told her she was bright, and she determinedly put herself through college. Attempting to escape the family, she married in her early twenties a man who was physically abusive. She asked him to leave, took him back, and a few years later divorced him. Working for years as an attendant for developmentally delayed individuals in an effort to give her own children educational and material opportunities she had lacked, she felt deeply disappointed that they wanted limited contact with her after leaving home. Instead, they blamed her for not divorcing their father sooner. Over the course of several years, she had seen therapists and psychiatrists but found CBT, nondirective therapy, and medication unhelpful with her chronic feelings of depression, shame, and low self-esteem.
>
> When asked about her spiritual life, she reported that she had grown up nominally Catholic, then experienced "grace" in a charismatic Protestant church, where worship gave her "freedom from my demons." She subsequently became interested in theology, and later in life thrived in seminary, for a while considering a Ph.D. However, her sensitivity to criticism prevented her from going into parish ministry and discouraged her from further graduate work. At the time she came for treatment, she was somewhat isolated, living in elderly

housing, uninvolved with a church or group of friends. She felt distant from God, unable to understand why he had allowed her to become so "defective."

She presented as a bright, somewhat cautious woman who appeared older than her stated age, sardonic at times but capable of warmth, and interested in the interviewer.

The initial diagnosis was chronic depression (dysthymia) related to trauma, with self-defeating personality traits. The formulation included her faith as both a potential resource and a source of distress.

Treatment initially focused on establishing a therapeutic alliance with a woman whose fragile sense of trust imperiled her ability to hope. Over months, weekly sessions stimulated both expectations of her therapist and traumatic memories of her mother beating her as a child. She came to feel more angry with God and sad at losing what had been a sustaining connection with Him.

Recognizing the importance of her struggles with hope, morality (shame), and her relationship with ultimate authority, her therapist (1) encouraged integration of her early traumatic experiences into her current self, through gentle, exploratory psychotherapy and referral to an adjunctive group on recovery from trauma; (2) examined how she had come to judge herself so harshly, and ways she could find forgiveness; (3) considered with her the fate of her spiritual life, with a view to recovering communication with God.

At times, when memories surfaced of her abusive past, she continued to feel overwhelmed and hopeless with suicidal ideation. However, as she came to feel more accepted and forgiven by her therapist, she was more able to use insight into how trauma had affected her and to become more forgiving of herself. Her difficulty forgiving God led her to discussion in therapy of the biblical character of Job, whose demand to see God sustained him through suffering. Cognitive disputation over scriptures she used to show predestination helped her to see that she was choosing a dark, fatalistic theology for emotional reasons. After joining a small group of other believers, she recovered her ability to pray about how God had viewed her, her life, and her damaged relationships with her children.

Helping this patient to deal with the ongoing impact of her trauma required her therapist to confront her cognitive distortions, promote forgiveness, and help her reenlist outside resources for connecting with God.

Perfectionism

Many individuals who have not been abused, but have been exposed to critical expectations respond by becoming overly exacting of themselves. Feeling unable to measure up, they may push themselves to perform, in a vain search for recognition and love. Disappointment, with attendant feelings of rejection and self-doubt can generalize to their feelings about God, who has expectations of them but has not chosen to protect them from disappointment. Humanistic approaches may help them identify with other values and to feel less grimly driven. CBT may help them work with their concept of God, and IPT or spiritual direction can help them explore the nature of that relationship.

> A 35-year-old married mother of two presented with worsening tearfulness, feelings of inadequacy, and anxiety. She had grown up compulsive about achieving high grades, winning in sports, and remaining thin. As a student in an elite college, she was attracted to students in a religious campus group because they seemed happy, and eventually adopted their faith as a central focus of her life. Temperamentally sensitive and introspective, she reported always wanting greater

closeness with her preoccupied CEO father and anxious mother, who always seemed to expect more from her. She had been briefly suicidal when she abandoned a promising religiously oriented career because a trusted mentor sexually assaulted her. At the time she came for treatment, her church's sermons had come to seem judgmental, and God critical and distant.

Treatment included medication, supportive and insight-oriented psychotherapy, and a focus on her spiritual life (which remained for her a major source of identity and meaning, if not of hope or grace). A discussion in therapy of how her core beliefs differed from the "you should" messages she heard weekly from the pulpit led her to visit other congregations. As she came to value more personal intimacy with God and creative expressions for her faith, she found a church that emphasized these. Although she remained vulnerable to low moods when engaged in self-criticism, for example about her parenting, she began to describe feeling "delight" in her children, and the experience of being "delighted in" by God. A few years into treatment, she was more open and forgiving toward herself in part because these attitudes were present in her new church and its pastor.

The therapist addressed this patient's oppressive sense of disapproval by God by helping her to understand its origins in her relationship to parental representations, by helping her reassess and act on her core beliefs about God, and by helping her find others in her religious community who could represent God to her in a way more consistent with them. Specifically, he helped her look for Christians who were more positive than Puritanical, and more focused on how to accept what God wants to give than on how to meet his expectations so as to avoid punishment. This required him to attend carefully to his own religious countertransference, so as not to overly influence her on the basis of his own beliefs.

Negative Identity

Other individuals respond to criticism by becoming defensive and expecting mistreatment. When conflicts over perceived slights lead to further rejection and isolation, they can feel defective, purposeless, even hopeless. Spiritual approaches can be difficult to implement because of the antagonism of these individuals toward authority, but a humanistic, positive emphasis on enhancing their resilience can be disarming.

> A 55-year-old divorced bright but opinionated office worker presented a long history of conflicts with authorities such as physicians and bosses. Crises led to repeated job changes and periods during which she briefly felt desperate and suicidal. She showed an ambivalent attitude toward her psychiatrist, wanting to learn personal details about his life, but to meet only infrequently. Examples of mistreatment by others in her current life were preferred as topics over the way her experience with controlling, critical parents might be affecting her behavior and perspective. She did, however, respond to her therapist's interest in more positive aspects of her life, such as a love of European literature and generosity to her old friends. Although proud of being an atheist, she one day admitted she had been enjoying attending a diverse church whose pastor she had met in another context. Her psychiatrist had not raised the topic of spirituality, but he wondered whether this had transference implications, as she has noted his interest in the area from his books.

A 60-year-old married Jewish antique dealer presented with chronic unhappiness, somatic preoccupation, and accounts of having survived two serious motor vehicle accidents and cancer. He came at his wife's insistence, with whom he described a strained relationship, and volunteered that he had been "emasculated" by his mother and first wife. Dyslexic as a child, he had focused on working hard in a niche that would provide a respectable income and home but now found that he had few other sources of pleasure or joy. In sessions he recounted his troubles, then asked provocative questions that reflected both his sense of himself and his need to be heard: "Do I bore you?" "Have you ever seen a case like mine?" "Don't you have any other medication for me?" "I don't expect to live much longer." He viewed himself as spared by God in his latest accident, but "for no reason." While he showed little interest in how his cynical perspective on himself and life might have developed and could change, he did appreciate being heard, took up a suggestion to visit his new grandchild, and became curious about what his therapist could see in his life that he could not see himself. His therapist's mirroring seemed to help him glimpse a more positive vision of himself in relation to the larger world.

Self-Sacrifice

Yet another way of responding to adversity is by sacrificing one's own interests in a misguided effort to find love or acceptance. The resulting depletion, feelings of inadequacy, and submerged anger can then present as guilt, self-doubt, rejection, and at times hopelessness. Many individuals feel a religious mandate to self-sacrifice, even though they may have consciously rejected the faith of their childhood. Spiritual approaches directed to clarifying what they believe, what gives them worth, and who accepts them as they are can foster both insight and comfort. Twelve Step approaches that address the grandiosity, compulsivity, and ineffective nature of codependent or masochistic self-sacrifice can also be useful for individuals who are willing to relinquish control to a Higher Power.

> A 50-year-old architect came for treatment for depression related to his complicated relationships with women. Though separated for years from his wife, he regularly argued with her over how much he should support her. He would initially insist that she work, then capitulate to her demands, then feel defeated, overextended, and resentful. Periodic involvement with other women provided additional reasons for his wife to accuse him of being incapable of commitment and for him to suspect her of being right. Exploration of his earlier relationships with women led to memories of his mother "demanding perfection" of all the children and, during adolescence, setting him up for beatings by his father when he would come in after hours. He described his mother as a rigid, insecure woman who emphasized duty, self-denial, and stoicism reinforced by Catholic teaching. As an adolescent he dealt with feelings of shame and self-doubt by rebelling against the family's Catholicism, often in secretive ways. He also kept secret being sexually abused during high school by a Catholic priest whom his mother had welcomed into their home.
>
> Insight-oriented treatment helped him to recognize the sources of his shame and insecurity, as well as maladaptive ways he tended to experience and deal with guilt and anger. Eventually, he was able to set effective limits on his wife's demands. He also achieved significant reconciliation with his mother when she apologized for her harsh treatment of him as an adolescent. He then asked his therapist for help to resolve ways that the family priest's sexual abuse continued to confuse him in his quest for sustainable spiritual values.

These examples illustrate both the changing priorities for clinicians addressing depressive concerns over time, and the place of spiritually oriented approaches in dealing with differing patterns of depressive vulnerability: cognitive and behavioral interventions that foster integration of the self with the larger context for hopelessness in the trauma survivor or desperate perfectionistic patient; an interpersonal focus or spiritual direction for the perfectionistic or self-sacrificing patient feeling isolated or rejected by God; a humanistic, positive psychology emphasis for despairing individuals with a negative identity and others who feel life is empty and meaningless; forgiveness-oriented approaches for the trauma survivor, and so on. A therapist may need to use different approaches within a single session, as one patient concern gives place to another.

> A trauma survivor whose faith had been an important source of comfort began the session by reporting on suicidal ideation she had during the week. She had experienced this when she was alone and thinking about her estrangement from family members who had a grievance against her. When the therapist asked if she had felt hopeless about being forgiven, she responded that she felt destined by God to suffer. Moving from an integrative and forgiveness-promoting approach to a cognitive one, he then asked whether she read about individuals in the scriptures having no choice in the face of God's action. She indicated that she felt overwhelmed by the idea that she might have had a choice, and by what she had lost as a result. Following her lead back to these relationships, he then encouraged her to grieve her hopes for them, so that she could make the best of what was realistically left—using an existential and an interpersonal approach.

IDENTIFYING GOALS OF SPIRITUAL CARE

As we have just seen, the urgency of depressive concerns can help determine their priority for receiving clinical attention and, therefore, for implementing spiritually oriented approaches. But what should be the goals of these approaches? To provide psychological support? To address a specific spiritual need, or relieve spiritual distress? To foster spiritual health, for example by removing obstacles to receiving spiritual resources or by repairing damage done by depression to faith? Consider circumstances under which each of these could be appropriate: In the first instance, a troubled relationship with God in a religious patient, or sense of meaninglessness could be thought of as problems amenable to being addressed on a psychological level. However, other forms of spiritual distress or need are less completely comprehensible in psychological terms. Depressed individuals, whether they consider themselves spiritual or not, may need spiritually oriented assistance in deciding whether and how to live, and where to find forgiveness. To treat these questions as epiphenomena of more basic psychological processes rather than as spiritual needs in their own right is to trivialize the patient's relationship to the larger universe. Finally, spiritually oriented approaches can serve primarily to enhance spiritual health, and to reduce vulnerability to depressive relapse. Consider for example the change fostered over time by Twelve Step Programs. In these programs of recovery, spirituality is not simply a means to sobriety, or even to living more comfortably, but a way of living more responsibly connected to other people and to God. From a religious perspective, spiritual growth, for all its psychological benefits, is not simply a means to better mental health.* A relationship with God is potentially all consuming and, if taken seriously, will be challenging as well as comforting. As a result, the clinician who adopts a spiritually oriented approach needs to think carefully with his patient about the goals of the care he is intending to provide and about his role in doing so as a therapist.

Defining the Therapist's Role

Even if a depressed individual needs spiritual care, how is it the role of a *therapist* to provide more than spiritual first aid and reassurance that the spiritual dimension of his life is being taken into account? Elsewhere, I have distinguished four possible roles of a psychotherapist in approaching spiritual problems (such as a crisis of faith, paralyzing guilt, or religious objections to taking medication).†

In the most familiar and straightforward of these, a therapist would acknowledge the problem, but limit discussion to its psychological (or strictly medical) dimension. For example, he might focus on how the problem is interfering with the patient's

---

* Shuman and Meador (2003).
† Peteet (1994).

care, or address a patient's anger at God by examining his relationship with other authority figures in the patient's life.

A second possible approach would be to clarify the spiritual as well as the psychological aspects of the problem, suggest resources for dealing with the former, and consider working with an outside resource such as a religious community or other authority. This might include enlisting a hospital chaplain or clergy person to offer needed spiritual help, or referring a patient to a therapist of a similar tradition. It could also include referral to organized programs that integrate beliefs and emotions, such as religiously/spiritually based cognitive behavioral or Twelve Step Programs.

In a third approach, one would aim to address the problem indirectly using the patient's own philosophy of life within the treatment. This might include exploring ways the patient can make better use of his resources and tradition (for example, by examining a range of beliefs within the patient's own denomination, or misconceptions about the spiritual nature of AA).

A fourth approach would be to address the problem directly together using a shared perspective, ranging from the therapist's agreement on the importance of hope, meaning, world view, or a caring community to the prescriptive use of shared values, beliefs, or practices (e.g., meditation or scripture) in the treatment. This fourth approach requires particularly careful attention to transference, countertransference, boundary, and consent issues.

A number of factors are relevant in deciding which of these approaches to take. The first is the patient's need—whether for growth, adjustment, or problem solving. This in turn influences the nature, primary aims, and timing of the work—for example, psychological insight into a maladaptive pattern or resolution of a conflict. These in turn influence the degree of direct support needed and the amount of interpersonal closeness that is appropriate. Additional factors include the patient's existential concerns—for example, related to hope, or identity—and the spiritual options under consideration; the importance of spirituality in his life; his presenting problem and attitude toward treatment; the concern of the patient to integrate psychological with other perspectives; the availability of outside philosophical or spiritual resources; and the therapist's own knowledge and preferred style. Dual relationships, for example being a treater as well as a fellow member of the same religious community, complicate the transference, countertransference, and boundary aspects of taking one or another approach.

Considering the Impact of the Patient and Therapist's World View

Patient and therapist world views shape to a considerable degree how they approach existential dilemmas having to do with identity, hope, meaning/purpose, morality, and attitudes toward autonomy in relation to authority.[*] An atheist is likely to experience these differently from one who believes life is

---
[*] Peteet (2004).

most fully lived in relationship to a personal God. A Hindu or Buddhist committed to acceptance of suffering and/or to future relief of suffering through rebirth might differ in his approach from a Christian who looks for the redemptive value of suffering. (What am I supposed to learn about myself and my relationship to God from this?) A patient who is discouraged and overwhelmed by adversity, but has a strong belief that God cares for her is likely to want support in searching for a way to draw upon, and be inspired by this faith. A patient whose adversity sparks deeper, depressive doubts that corrode her convictions about God may need an interpersonal focus on their relationship. A patient with a harsh, introjected representation of God, who believes that he is angry with her over her failings may need a dynamically oriented exploration of these feelings and help comparing them in a cognitive behavioral way with the tenets of her faith. And a patient who believes that God does not exist may need support in dealing with anger that lacks a target, and a gentle, humanistic approach to help him find positive objects and ideals with which he can identify.

A therapist's own world view can also influence the direction of the work adversely, in several ways. If he shares his patient's general world view, he may inadvertently leave unexplored important beliefs of his patient on the assumption that he understands them already. If he holds a different world view which he feels his patient would benefit from adopting, he may consciously or unconsciously encourage this, whether by suggesting that the patient is too religious, or not religious enough. Religiously based countertransference can of course be nuanced in much more complex ways.[*,†]

A third way in which world view influences the treatment approach is through the availability of religious and spiritual resources. Does the patient have a faith community? What is his relationship to it? What is the nature of the community? Is the community a good fit for the patient in terms of theology, style of worship, ability to reach care for individuals with doubts and/or major emotional needs? For example, does it emphasize small groups, worship, retreats, service, and/or formal pastoral counseling that the patient could try to use? Has he tried them, and with what effect? If the patient's beliefs and needs seem to match the community's resources, the therapist can address the patient's resistance to more active participation, as he might for a patient needing to engage AA more actively in order to consolidate his sobriety. If not, he can help the patient explore other options within his tradition. If the community seems to be having a toxic effect on the patient, he may need to make this explicit.

> A 40-year-old married office worker and artist came for help in dealing with Internet pornography addiction and chronic depression. As an evangelical Christian, he was distressed when his new church chose a more liberal pastor who paid less attention to parishioners' personal struggles. His therapist confronted his tendency to become

---

[*] Abernathy and Lancia (1998).
[†] Peteet (2004).

paralyzed by feeling a victim and encouraged him to consider other churches that could better meet his and his family's needs.

Respecting Boundaries

When and how should a therapist disclose his own world view? As in dealing with other kinds of self-disclosure, a therapist will want to understand what the patient's request means and whether it serves the patient.[*] Answering a religious patient's question about whether his therapist believes in God can be an important element in achieving informed consent, if he needs to know whether he can trust his therapist's values. On the other hand, answering the same question from a provocative patient could serve to divert attention from an important therapeutic issue into an unproductive theological discussion.

Should one ever treat a member of his own congregation? Agree to pray, or discuss scripture with a patient? Risks attend engaging in dual relationships and roles, but as Gutheil and Gabbard[†] point out, a "boundary crossing," a descriptive term, differs from a "boundary violation," which represents a harmful crossing, or transgression of a boundary. As they further note, the specific impact of a boundary crossing can only be assessed by careful attention to the clinical context. For example, it may be coercive and unethical to suggest prayer, but depending on the clinical context it may be therapeutic to accept a patient's request

---

[*] Peteet (2004).
[†] Gutheil and Gabbard (1993, 1998).

to pray together, if a therapist can do so sincerely and with a clear understanding of how it advances the goals of the therapy. In dealing with situations in which the patient has another relationship with the therapist (e.g., is a fellow congregant), anticipating, discussing, and maintaining confidentiality is crucial.

Avoiding Pitfalls

Clinicians can devote either too little or too much attention to spirituality in treating depression. There may be several reasons for neglecting the spiritual dimension of patients' experience. Asking about and exploring this area can seem overly time-consuming for a busy clinician. Therapists unfamiliar with the patient's tradition may be unsure what to ask. Inexperienced clinicians may not recognize connections between the patient's spiritual and emotional struggles, and the therapeutic potential of addressing them. They may also miss opportunities because of reliance on a single, favored paradigm. For example, use of a medical paradigm can lead to a focus on symptoms rather than underlying conflicts, use of a psychological paradigm to a focus on dynamic explanations rather than on moral or spiritual realities, and use of an existential paradigm to a focus on coping with life challenges ("finding meaning") rather than on the transforming potential of the individual's spirituality. A clinician's concern with boundaries, and with keeping his own spirituality private may inhibit discussion that questions what he believes. Finally, antireligious bias, or unresolved spiritual questions can lead a therapist to avoid or de-emphasize these issues.

Potential consequences of neglecting the spiritual dimension of depression include a flattening of perspective, lack of positive vision, and missed opportunities to address important sources of distress such as loss of connection with God.

Clinicians can also devote too much attention to spiritual issues. The impetus may come from patients who understand their problems primarily in these terms. Some patients are reluctant to accept that they need medication, instead believing they need to have more faith. Some prefer to focus on a spiritual belief or practice rather than to face their need to change self-defeating patterns. Still others may focus on being controlled or cursed by God rather than on the choices that are available to them.

Therapists may also devote too much attention to spiritual issues for reasons of their own. They may be drawn too far into a patient's unbalanced perception of his problem because of an unresolved, parallel personal struggle. They may feel that a spiritual practice, perspective, or experience that has been useful to them would also help the patient. Or they may be vulnerable to engaging in unproductive theological debate due to countertransference—for example, from an unconscious desire to liberate a younger patient from views they rejected in separating from their family of origin. Potential consequences of overemphasizing spirituality in treatment include diverting attention from the patient's emotional needs and conflicts, devaluing other, more appropriate sources of spiritual care such as a pastor, and exerting undue influence on a patient who needs to find his own way.

Avoiding the Scilla of neglect and the Charybdis of overemphasis requires clinical judgment, and at times consultation with colleagues. Some useful questions to ask in finding the best approach are:

- What is the patient's primary need from me as a therapist?
- What are the patient's spiritual problems and resources?
- What is the contribution of the patient's spiritual problems to his depression?
- What is the potential contribution of their spiritual resources in combating it?
- What outside sources of spiritual help are available, and what blocks the patient from being able to make use of them?
- Should these blocks be a focus of the treatment?
- What are the pros and cons of taking on the role of spiritual provider in the therapy?
- Am I prepared to reveal my own spiritual perspective, if asked, and at what cost to me and to the therapy?

Addressing Resistance to Treatment

In the previous chapter, we identified some spiritual resistances to treatment generally, and to interventions such as medication specifically. General fears that a clinical approach will undermine faith can often be allayed by collaboration between referring clergy and clinicians. Both may find it helpful to use the analogy of other medical illnesses for which the patient would not hesitate to take prescribed medication (in addition to praying for recovery). A pragmatic attitude that encourages a trial of medication alongside other approaches may have more chance of acceptance than one that is more dogmatic. A clinician who is conversant with the patient's tradition of belief can also recruit wisdom from that tradition to reinforce cognitive behavioral interventions and to encourage the practice of spiritual disciplines which are likely to have therapeutic effects—such as engaging with others on what is most meaningful in life, being inspired by reading, or engaging in service.

In summary, we have considered here how a therapist can help depressed individuals who experience the universe as dark and meaningless, life as joyless and empty of hope, and themselves as inadequate or guilty. We have suggested that to survive the worst of his despair, a depressed patient may need to rely on the experience of his therapist and of others caring for him. Having survived, he then needs help to acknowledge and bear real losses, correct his distorted perspective, and maintain a vital connection to the larger world. For a mystically oriented individual, this may take the form of sensing God's presence even when down; for an individual in early recovery from addiction, keeping a focus outside himself; for a ritually oriented individual, finding a way to overcome his disillusionment with the church; and for a spiritually skeptical individual, a way to live consistent with his ideals. We have examined two major ways in which a therapist can help foster such connections. He can help the patient to address cognitive, characterologic, or traumatic obstacles to reengaging God, his ideals, or the experience of beauty. He can also, while attending to balance and taking care to serve the patient's needs rather than his own, encourage the patient in his search for other, outside resources that are capable of sustaining, and even of transforming his experience and outlook, recognizing that depressive struggles related to particular existential concerns benefit from specific spiritual approaches (Table 4.1). Finally, we have reviewed a number of practical considerations involved in implementing an integrated approach: deciding on priorities and approaches to spiritual care (to addressing issues such as trauma, perfectionism, negative self-identity, or self-sacrifice), defining the clinician's role, taking into account the patient's and the clinician's world view, respecting boundaries, and avoiding common pitfalls.

References

Abernathy, A.D., & Lancia, J.J. (1998). Religion and the psychotherapeutic relationship. Transferential and countertransferential dimensions. *J Psychother Pract Res,* 7, 281–289.

Benner, D.G. (2005). Intensive soul care: Integrating psychotherapy and spiritual direction. In L. Sperry & E.P. Shafranske (Eds.), *Spiritually Oriented Psychotherapy*. Washington, DC: American Psychological Association, pp. 287–306.

Breitbart, W. (2002). Spirituality and meaning in supportive care: Spirituality- and meaning-centered group psychotherapy interventions in advanced cancer. *Support Care Cancer,* 10, 272–280.

Cole, B., & Pargament, K. (1999). Re-creating your life: A spiritual/psychotherapeutic intervention for people diagnosed with cancer. *Psycho-oncology,* 8, 395–407.

Cooper, L.A., Brown, C., Vu, H.T., Ford, D.E., & Powe, N.R. (2001). How important is intrinsic spirituality in depression care? A comparison of white and African American primary care patients. *J Gen Intern Med,* 16, 634–638.

Cooper, L.A., Brown, C., Vu, H.T., Palenchar, D.R., Gonzales, J.J., Ford, D.E., et al. (2000). Primary care patients' opinions regarding the importance of various aspects of care for depression. *Gen Hosp Psychiatry,* 22, 163–173.

Elkins, D.N. (2005). A humanistic approach to spiritually oriented psychotherapy. In L. Sperry and E.P. Shafranske (Eds.), *Spiritually Oriented Psychotherapy.* Washington, DC: American Psychological Association, pp. 131–152.

Folkman, S., & Greer, S. (2000). Promoting psychological well-being in the face of serious illness: When theory, research and practice inform each other. *Psycho-Oncology,* 9, 11–19.

Frankl, V.E. (1970). *The Will to Meaning: Foundations and Applications of Logotherapy.* New York: New American Library.

Gutheil, T.G., & Gabbard, G.O. (1993). The concept of boundaries in clinical practice: Theoretical and risk-management dimensions. *Am J Psychiatry,* 150, 188–196.

Gutheil, T.G., & Gabbard, G.O. (1998). Misuses and misunderstandings of boundary theory in clinical and regulatory settings. *Am J Psychiatry,* 155, 409–414.

Hodge, D.R. (2006). Spiritually modified cognitive therapy: A review of the literature. *Soc Work,* 51, 157–166.

Klerman, G.L. (1984). *Interpersonal Psychotherapy of Depression.* New York: Basic Books.

Levenson, M.R., Aldwin, C.M., & Yancura, L. (2006). Positive emotional change: Mediating effects of forgiveness and spirituality. *Explore (NY),* 2, 498–508.

Ma, S.H., & Teasdale, J.D. (2004). Mindfulness-based cognitive therapy for depression: Replication and exploration of differential relapse prevention effects. *J Consult Clin Psychol,* 72, 31–40.

Miller, D.K., Chibnall, J.T., Videen, S.D., & Duckro, N. (2005). Supportive-affective group experience for persons with life-threatening illness: Reducing spiritual, psychological, and death-related distress in dying patients. *J Palliat Med,* 8, 333–343.

Miller, L. (2005). Interpersonal psychotherapy from a spiritual perspective. In L. Sperry and E.P. Shafranske (Eds.), *Spiritually Oriented Psychotherapy.* Washington, DC, American Psychological Association, pp. 153–176.

Nielsen, S.L., Johnson, W.B., & Ellis, A. (2001). *Counseling and Psychotherapy with Religious Persons: A Rational Emotive Behavior Therapy Approach.* Mahwah, NJ: L. Erlbaum Associates.

Peteet, J.R. (1993). A closer look at the role of a spiritual approach in addictions treatment. *J Subst Abuse Treat,* 10, 263–267.

Peteet, J.R. (1994). Approaching spiritual issues in psychotherapy: A conceptual framework. *J Psychotherapy Pract Res,* 3, 237–245.

Peteet, J.R. (2004). Therapeutic implications of world view. In A.J. Josephson & J.R. Peteet (Eds.), *Handbook of Spirituality and World View in Clinical Practice.* Washington, DC: American Psychiatric Publishing, Inc., pp. 47–59.

Peterson, C., & Seligman, M.E.P. (2004). *Character Strengths and Virtues: A Handbook and Classification.* Washington, DC; New York: American Psychological Association; Oxford University Press.

Probst, L.R., Ostrom, R., Watkins, P., Dan, T., & Mashburn, D. (1992). Comparative efficacy of religious and nonreligious cognitive therapy for the treatment of depression in religious individuals. *J Counseling Consult Psychol,* 69, 94–103.

Richards, S. (2005). Theistic integrative psychotherapy. In L. Sperry & E.P. Shafranske (Eds.), *Spiritually Oriented Psychotherapy.* Washington, DC: American Psychological Association, pp. 259–285.

Rizzuto, A.-M. (1979). *The Birth of the Living God: A Psychoanalytic Study.* Chicago: University of Chicago Press.

Segal, Z.V., Williams, J.M.G., & Teasdale, J.D. (2002). *Mindfulness-Based Cognitive Therapy for Depression: A New Approach to Preventing Relapse.* New York: Guilford Press.

Seligman, M.E., Steen, T.A., Park, N., & Peterson, C. (2005). Positive psychology progress: Empirical validation of interventions. *Am Psychol,* 60, 410–421.

Shafranske, E.P. (2005). A psychoanalytic approach to spiritually oriented psychotherapy. In L. Sperry & E.P. Shafranske (Eds.), *Spiritually Oriented Psychotherapy.* Washington, DC: American Psychological Association, pp. 105–130.

Shuman, J.J., & Meador, K.G. (2003). *Heal Thyself: Spirituality, Medicine, and the Distortion of Christianity.* New York: Oxford University Press.

Sperry, L. (2005). Integrative spiritually oriented psychotherapy. In L. Sperry & E.P. Shafranske (Eds.), *Spiritually Oriented Psychotherapy.* Washington, DC: American Psychological Association, pp. 307–329.

Tan, S., & Johnson, W.B. (2005). Spiritually oriented cognitive-behavioral therapy. In L. Sperry & E.P. Shafranske (Eds.), *Spiritually Oriented Psychotherapy.* Washington, DC: American Psychological Association, pp. 77–103.

Teasdale, J.D., Segal, Z.V., Williams, J.M.G., Ridgeway, V.A., Soulsby, J.M., & Lau, M.A.. (2000). Prevention of relapse/recurrence in major depression by mindfulness-based cognitive therapy. *J Consult Clin Psychol,* 68, 615–623.

Wachholtz, A.B., & Pargament, K. (2005). Is spirituality a critical ingredient of meditation? Comparing the effects of spiritual meditation, secular meditation, and relaxation on spiritual, psychological, cardiac, and pain outcomes. *J Behav Med,* 28, 369–384.

Worthington, E.L., Mazzeo, S.E., & Canter, D.E. (2005). Forgiveness-promoting approach: Helping clients reach forgiveness through using a longer model that teaches reconciliation. In L. Sperry & E.P. Shafranske (Eds.), *Spiritually Oriented Psychotherapy.* Washington, DC: American Psychological Association, 235–257.

5 Suicide

O, that this too too solid flesh would melt,
Thaw and resolve itself into a dew!
Or that the Everlasting had not fix'd
His canon 'gainst self-slaughter. O God, O God.[*]

William Shakespeare, *Hamlet*

Suicide, the most feared complication of depression, is responsible for over 30,000 deaths annually in the United States.

What is the relationship between spirituality and this desperate act? In what follows I examine (1) evidence that religion and spirituality influence suicide; (2) how clinicians can usefully take this relationship into account in assessing and reducing suicide risk; (3) ways of bringing spiritual resources to bear in dealing with the concerns of suicidal individuals; and (4) approaches to helping families and friends heal in the aftermath of a completed suicide.

---
[*] Thompson and Taylor (2006).

Studies of Suicide and Spirituality

Durkheim,[*] in his sociological study *Suicide,* argued that religion deters suicide by enhancing social integration. Subsequent research has challenged Durkheim's findings by suggesting that the religious involvement of individuals may be more important than the religious affiliations of populations. Koenig,[†] in a comprehensive review of research published prior to 2000, found that 57 of 68 studies showed an inverse relationship between religious involvement and suicide. Subsequent literature, reviewed by Moreira-Almeida et al. in 2006,[‡] has continued to show an inverse relationship between religiosity and suicide in the behavior of clinical populations,[§] in the attitudes of adolescents toward suicide,[¶,**] in the suicidal ideation of elderly,[††] and in the acceptance of euthanasia and physician-assisted suicide among patients,[‡‡] physicians,[§§] and the general public.[¶¶]

Mechanisms that have been proposed for mediating this relationship involve social support and cohesion; beliefs that provide a cognitive framework for buffering stress, reasons to live,

---

[*] Durkheim (1897/1951).
[†] Koenig (2001).
[‡] Moreira-Almeida et al. (2006).
[§] Dervic et al. (2004, 2006).
[¶] Nonnemaker et al. (2003).
[**] Eskin (2004).
[††] Cook et al. (2002).
[‡‡] O'Mahony et al. (2005).
[§§] Douglas et al. (2001).
[¶¶] O'Neill et al. (2003).

or moral objections to suicide (such as responsibilities to one's family); a relationship to a loving God; and religious practices such as meditation.

What evidence exists about the relative importance of these factors? Several studies suggest that a commitment to a set of personal religious beliefs appears to be more significant than social cohesiveness per se. Similar to Walker et al.'s[*] study of college students, two studies of adolescent suicide[†,‡] point to the importance of intrinsic religiosity (defined as religious commitment) and religious influence (the degree to which subjects reported using their religious/spiritual beliefs to decide whether to engage in certain behaviors). Rasic et al.'s[§] description of almost 37,000 participants in the Canadian Community Health Survey indicated that regular attendance at religious services, but not reported spirituality, was associated with a decreased risk of suicide. Dervic et al.'s[¶] study of psychiatric inpatients suggests that religion may protect against suicide by reducing aggression and providing moral objections to suicide. Lizardi et al.[**] found moral objections to suicide acting independently as a deterrent. In a Swiss population of 145 psychiatric patients, Huguelet et al.[††]

---

[*] Walker et al. (2005).
[†] Greening and Stoppelbein (2002).
[‡] Rew et al. (2001).
[§] Rasic et al. (2009).
[¶] Dervic et al. (2004).
[**] Lizardi et al. (2008).
[††] Huguelet et al. (2007).

found that, while religiousness was not associated with suicide attempts, 25 percent reported a protective effect (primarily through ethical objections and religious coping), and that one in ten reported an incentive role (both through negative religious ideas and through the hope of something better after death). Epidemiologic studies have found lower rates of suicide among Muslims and Christians than among Hindus, Sikhs, Buddhists, or Jews.[*] Interestingly, a cross-sectional study of 1456 Native Americans[†] found that commitment to neither Christianity nor cultural spirituality, as measured by beliefs, was correlated with suicide attempts. However, the authors found that commitment to cultural spirituality as measured by "spiritual orientation" showed a significant deterrent effect. Spiritually oriented individuals endorsed statements such as: "I am in harmony with all living things"; "I feel connected with other people in life"; "I follow the Red Road [the spiritual path prescribed by tribal tradition]"; "When I need to return to balance, I know what to do"; "I feel like I am living the right way"; and "I am a person of integrity." The phenomena recognized by these statements highlight the importance of affect, identity, and morality.

While research has yet to clearly specify the ways that religion/spirituality influence suicide, clinical experience suggests several ways to take its influence into account. Among

---

[*] De Leo (2002).

[†] Garroutte et al. (2003).

the most important are in the assessment and reduction of suicide risk.

Suicide Assessment and Prevention

The fact that many individuals who commit suicide saw a clinician shortly beforehand suggests that they may have been looking for help[*]—perhaps as a last attempt to connect with someone who cares. In addition to questions about suicidal thoughts, plans, means, and prior attempts, an understanding of the patient's spirituality can help to identify those at risk and suggest ways to intervene—particularly in relation to hope, guilt, and beliefs about suicide and life after death.

HOPE

Hopelessness strongly predicts suicide.[†] A clinician exploring a depressed patient's hopes would want to know: What has made his or her life worth living?[‡] How does he see the future? Do disappointments in achieving valued goals mean that these goals need to be reassessed? What resources are available for putting unrealistic hopes into a larger context?

> A 30-year-old Asian graduate student tempted to take an overdose of pills explained that she felt hopeless about meeting her parents' expectations that she excel academically. Assessing her risk involved exploring

---

[*] Hirshfeld and Russell (1997).
[†] Beck et al. (1985).
[‡] Malone et al. (2000).

whether she could clarify her core values as distinct from those of her parents, and engage in family therapy. Determining whether she and her parents shared a faith was an integral part of this assessment. On the one hand, as a Christian she felt that she been unable to meet God's expectations as well as her parents.' On the other hand, her parents' faith provided a basis for them to accept her as belonging to God, rather than to them, and to discuss together what might be even more important than their own personal hopes for her life.

Guilt

Is a depressed patient feeling so guilty that he deserves to die? Does he show a pattern of self-blame in the face of adversity? Is he capable of using insight gained from therapy, or from a pastor that his/her guilt may be irrational? Or is this an uncharacteristic, fixed, and perhaps even delusional symptom that requires pharmacological intervention or electroconvulsive therapy (ECT)? What ultimately grounds his sense of worth? Does he have a way to find forgiveness? How effective is it?

Beliefs About Suicide and Life After Death

What does the patient believe about the morality of taking one's life? About what happens after death?[*] Does he believe he will be punished (or rewarded in the case of a terrorist[†]) for suicide

---

[*] Malone et al. (2000).
[†] Religiously motivated suicide, either expressing protest as in the case of Buddhist monks who immolated themselves during the Vietnam era, or implementing terror as in the case of suicide bombers in the Middle East, is an increasingly important phenomenon that is beyond the scope of this chapter.

in the next life? How concerned is he about the impact on survivors? Is he drawn to die by fantasies of reunion in an afterlife?[*]

Of interest here are not only the strength of the patient's depressive concerns, but also the ways in which the patient's spirituality is a potential resource, or a source of conflict. Consider four common possibilities:

1. The patient's depressive concerns (hopelessness, or guilt) have not penetrated to the patient's spirituality, but his spirituality is superficial and not a conscious influence in his life. A clinician will want to help the patient identify core values, but will not expect him to be able to hold onto them immediately, especially when feeling desperate.
2. The patient's depressive concerns have not penetrated his spirituality, and his sense of being loved by God or fearful of displeasing him by suicide are active deterrents. There may be ways to strengthen the patient's resistance to suicide, for example by clarifying these issues or by enlisting pastoral support. However, it is also possible to rely too heavily on a patient's spirituality. For example, a patient who believed God disapproved of suicide nevertheless decided he would forgive her for wanting to be with him.
3. The patient's depressive concerns have penetrated his spirituality, as reflected in active spiritual conflict. Examples include doubting whether God cares after allowing an

---

[*] Hendin (1991).

illness or a loss, and struggling to comprehend betrayal by a religious figure. A clinician would want to help the patient address both the spiritual as well as the emotional components of such conflicts to reduce their power.
4. The patient's depressive concerns have not only penetrated, but corroded his spirituality. Examples include the patient who has lost his faith, or who feels God cannot forgive him. While acknowledging the significance of these losses, a clinician would want to focus on treating such a patient's depression before attempting to help him recover his lost spiritual beliefs or experiences.

Problems in the patient's spiritual life may also add to his depressive vulnerability and suicide risk. Examples would include distress due to sexual abuse by a pastor, or to similar betrayal by another trusted religious figure. A therapist would want to address directly the spiritual impact of the experience and help the patient find a vision capable of sustaining him.

Treatment

Individuals who struggle with suicide need close attention to safety, including a focus on their self-destructive thoughts and behavior. They also need help with effective coping strategies, such as the ability to reach out to other people rather than act impulsively when overwhelmed. And they may need help with the existential and spiritual dimensions of their depressive concerns in the domains of identity, hope, meaning/purpose, morality, autonomy/authority, and connection.

IDENTITY

A public scandal may cause a respected businessman to become suicidal, and a disabling accident may put at risk an individual whose athleticism has been central to his sense of self. Similarly, the loss of a schizophrenic patient's delusional identity may put him at risk as he emerges from psychosis.

Helping patients to reexamine the commitments that have shaped who they are and want to be, and the larger context in which these commitments are rooted is to foster a spirituality that is engaged and a resource for transformation. We have earlier seen how narrative[*] and meaning-centered[†] approaches are examples.

> A 70-year-old retired Unitarian minister with pancreatic cancer said he wanted to die because he could no longer be of service. He explained, "If I believed there were an authority out there taking care of things to whom I was responsible, I would feel differently but I don't. I simply believe in service. When I can't continue to improve things, what's the point of going on?"
>
> His therapist explored why his recent incapacitation seemed to have invalidated a life of service and his worth to family and friends. Did his patient's humanistic world view require this conclusion, or was his counterdependent personality the more important factor? But rather than focusing on the relationship between his patient's counterdependence and his vulnerability to depression if not "productive," he drew

---

[*] Viederman and Perry (1980).
[†] Breitbart (2009).

attention to how his world view had grounded his identity and could continue to do so if he gave others the opportunity to serve him.

Hope

In addition to exploring the questions suggested above about what grounds a patient's hope, clinicians working with chronically suicidal individuals will want to understand what vital sources of trust and confidence have failed them. Trauma at the hand of early caregivers may have left them vulnerable to disintegration of basic trust, particularly when reactivated by a subsequent loss or betrayal. They may have lost hope for themselves, listening instead to old criticism that prevents their appreciating their accomplishments, their faith, or the possibility of learning from their mistakes.

At times, a faith community can provide crucial support in helping a trauma survivor to reconstruct his distorted and fragmented view of the world.

> A 30-year-old occupational therapist with a history of childhood sexual abuse felt suicidal when overwhelmed, often after working with young female patients. Therapy involved months of establishing trust in her therapist, but she also felt dependent on God for healing. Her therapist helped her to enlist support from her church in the form of honest prayer with her pastor and with members of a weekly small prayer and sharing group, having friends from church accompany her from difficult therapy sessions when she did not feel safe alone, and participating in a religiously based program for other survivors of similar trauma, lasting several months. As her trust in others and her

confidence in herself grew, episodes of feeling hopeless and suicidal became less frequent.

Meaning / Purpose

Suicidal individuals often question whether life has any meaning, or if it has enough to outweigh their pain. They may doubt if a God exists who could allow so much suffering.

It can help not only to join such patients in their quest for spiritual answers, but to help them foster a spirituality that is contemplative and attuned to larger realities, rather than distracted by proximate distress or impulses. Active appreciation of music, art, or nature, as well as prayer and worship can all help maintain self-transcendence, or a center of gravity beyond the self. Mindfulness has become integral to the most successful treatment for parasuicidal behavior, or dialectical behavior therapy (DBT).

> A 50-year-old, bright administrator with borderline personality disorder often felt demeaned by her boss at work, and periodically declared her intention to kill herself because her life was meaningless. Therapy devoted to helping her to understand the origins of her sensitivity to rejection and to call for help before acting on her suicidal urges was somewhat stabilizing, but she felt diminished by remaining dependent on mental health professionals. As an atheist she had always regarded spiritual practices as absurd, but found sustaining the experience of beauty that she shared with others in her Renaissance literature classes.

MORALITY

Spiritually oriented individuals who feel they do not deserve to live often suffer from irrational guilt that is embedded in an immature moral and spiritual perspective.

> As he approached retirement, a 65-year-old Protestant minister with obsessional traits developed an agitated depression marked by feelings that he had committed a sin that would send him to hell. He gradually improved with a combination of medication, psychotherapy supportive of his need for time to recover, mature theological responses from clerical friends, and appreciation by his wife and church of what he could still do for God.

Anger (often unconscious) can be an important element of suicidal fantasies and behavior. As the findings of Dervic's study[*] suggest, religion may help to deter suicide by reducing aggression (perhaps through providing means of achieving forgiveness), and by providing moral objections to suicide. Therapists of patients who struggle with rage directed inward and indirectly at others may find models and wisdom in the patient's faith for dealing more effectively with their resentments and frustration.

CONNECTION

It is common for a suicidal individual to feel alone, misunderstood, and rejected by everyone including God. If he had a sustaining relationship with God before becoming depressed, it

---

[*] Dervic et al. (2004).

may be useful to explore what happened. Does he assume God is judging him, and on what basis? How does he interpret scriptures such as the story of the prodigal son that present God as forgiving?

> A 30-year-old doctoral student in theology felt guilty, overwhelmed, and unable to sleep after revealing to her husband that she had become attracted to an admiring faculty mentor. Her husband, a pastor who had little interest in the academic life, said that he forgave her. A psychiatrist helped her to stabilize with medication, to clarify what she wanted for herself, and to explore the childhood roots of her wish to be accepted for being perfect. She also sought out a pastoral counselor, who as she accepted forgiveness from God and from her husband, helped them to improve their communication and achieve a renewed commitment to a shared ministry.

Of course, acutely suicidal individuals may lack the capacity to reach out to a pastor or therapist to respond in this way, or even to hold onto what is left of their relationship with God. Clinicians need to actively provide connections for such patients and help them identify other relationships that could help to take its place.

> A 32-year-old postdoctoral researcher presented for treatment after an attempt to hang himself while intoxicated. His history included the pursuit of career over interpersonal goals, and a propensity to drink under stress even though his father, a retired professor, had recently died from alcoholism. After rebelling against his Catholic upbringing, he had become an atheist who believed in the ability of science to create a better world. However, he had become increasingly

disillusioned with his lab chief, whom he had come to see as ruthlessly ambitious rather than supportive of his subordinates' work. At the time of his suicide attempt, he saw nothing worth living for, but after becoming sober began individual treatment. During a session, he noted books on spirituality and mental health in his therapist's office, and asked if he believed in God.

Losses and disappointments had intensified this patient's search for meaning and purpose and (like his father) he used alcohol to dull his pain. Now he looked for direction from his therapist, who tried to both help him grieve these losses and reformulate a view of the world that could provide sustained hope. In an effort to be transparent with a man who looked for honesty in authorities, the therapist crossed a boundary to acknowledge that he was a person of faith. At the same time, he took pains not to expect the patient to follow his lead toward belief in God. Instead, they discussed how he could find meaning and purpose in his relationships, activities, and commitments.

After becoming a father shortly thereafter, with an additional reason to live, the patient raised in therapy his dilemma about whether he could with integrity have his son baptized. His eventual decision to do so reflected both the dynamic nature of his ambivalence and the degree to which his depression had influenced his spirituality.

The Aftermath and Ways to Help

Family members and friends who survive a completed suicide often suffer from painful, unanswerable questions such as: Why did this happen? Could I have done something to prevent it? What kept him from confiding in me? How can this be fair? Where is he now? What gives my own life meaning?[*,†]

---

[*] Chance (1988).

[†] Fine (1997).

There are at least five ways a therapist can help individuals struggling with these questions. One is to help clarify the facts. It may be that the patient had not intended to die, or that he had expressed concerns that were unrelated to those of the survivor.

Second, a clinician can help the survivor understand the impact of the patient's psychiatric condition. For example, many people are unfamiliar with the way that severe depression can distort one's ability to see options and to make decisions. It can be helpful to hear from a mental health professional that suicide risk cannot be addressed unless the individual is willing to disclose it.

Third, a therapist can help individuals to bear the loss by reviewing and sharing it, and by encouraging participation in a bereavement group.

Fourth, a therapist can help individuals recognize and address specifically what the death means for them. Does it challenge strongly held, unreasonable assumptions that they should have been reason enough for the patient to live, or been able to protect him?

Fifth, therapists can help survivors to put the suicide of a loved one into larger perspective. Resolving the questions it has raised about the universe may involve accepting their limitations, arguing with God, rethinking suicide, reexamining their beliefs about what happens after death, and/or recognizing and finding forgiveness for their own failures to do what they should have done for the person. Religious authorities and sources of support can be important resources, but may not be readily available to individuals who have been alienated from institutional religion.

Finally, clinicians themselves struggle with feelings and questions about the meaning of the suicides that have touched their lives. Their ability to help patients and survivors deal with this challenge depends on their calling on sources of wisdom beyond themselves.

In summary, we have reviewed research indicating that religious involvement is inversely correlated with suicide and several possible reasons for this. We have seen how understanding patients' spirituality can help in assessing and reducing their risk of suicide when it is mediated by hopelessness, guilt, or beliefs about life after death. We have considered how clinicians can treat suicidal individuals by addressing their desperation and existential suffering in the domains of identity, hope, meaning/purpose, morality, and connection. And we have identified several ways that clinicians can help survivors with the spiritual dimension of their experience in the aftermath of a completed suicide.

References

Beck, A.T., Steer, R.A., Kovasc, M., & Garrison, B. (1985). Hopelessness and eventual suicide: A 10-year prospective study of patients hospitalized with suicidal ideation. *Am J Psychiatry,* 142, 559–563.

Breitbart, W., Rosenfeld, B., Gibson, C., Pessin, H., Poppito, S., Nelson, C., Tomarken, A., Timm, A.K., Berg, A., Jacobson, C., Sorger, B., Abbey, J., & Olden, M. (2009). Meaning-centered group psychotherapy for patients with advanced cancer: A pilot randomized controlled trial. *Psycho-Oncology,* 19, 21–28.

Chance, S. (1988). Surviving suicide. A journey to resolution. *Bull Menninger Clin,* 52, 30–39.

Cook, J.M., Pearson, J.L., Thompson, R., Black, B.S., & Rabins, P. (2002). Suicidality in older African Americans: Findings from the EPOCH study. *Am J Geriatr Psychiatry,* 10, 437–446.

De Leo, D. (2002). Struggling against suicide: The need for an integrative approach. *Crisis,* 23, 23–31.

Dervic, K., Oquendo, M.A., Currier, D., Grunebaum, M.F., Burke, A.K., & Mann, J.J. (2006). Moral objections to suicide: Can they counteract suicidality in patients with cluster B psychopathology? *J Clin Psychiatry,* 67, 620–625.

Dervic, K., Oquendo, M.A., Grunebaum, M.F., Ellis, S., Burke, A.K., & Mann, J.J. (2004). Religious affiliation and suicide attempt. *Am J Psychiatry,* 161, 2303–2308.

Douglas, C.D., Kerridge, I.H., Rainbird, K.J., McPhee, J.R., Hancock, L., & Spigelman, A.D. (2001). The intention to hasten death: A survey of attitudes and practices of surgeons in Australia. *Med J Aust,* 175, 511–515.

Durkheim, E. (1951). *Suicide, a Study in Sociology.* Glencoe, IL: Free Press.

Eskin, M. (2004). The effects of religious versus secular education on suicide ideation and suicidal attitudes in adolescents in Turkey. *Soc Psychiatry Psychiatr Epidemiol,* 39, 536–542.

Fine, C. (1997). *No Time to Say Goodbye: Surviving the Suicide of a Loved One.* New York: Doubleday.

Garroutte, E.M., Goldberg, J., Beals, J. Herrell, R., & Manson, S.M. (2003). Spirituality and attempted suicide among American Indians. *Soc Sci Med,* 56, 1571–1579.

Greening, L., & Stoppelbein, L. (2002). Religiosity, attributional style, and social support as psychosocial buffers for African American and white adolescents' perceived risk for suicide. *Suicide Life Threat Behav,* 32, 404–417.

Hendin, H. (1991). Psychodynamics of suicide, with particular reference to the young. *Am J Psychiatry,* 148, 1150–1158.

Hirschfeld, R.M., & Russell, J.M. (1997). Assessment and treatment of suicidal patients. *N Engl J Med,* 337, 910–915.

Huguelet, P., Mohr, S., Jung, V., Gillieron, C., Brandt, P.-Y., & Borras, L. (2007). Effect of religion on suicide attempts in outpatients with schizophrenia or schizo-affective disorders compared with inpatients with non-psychotic disorders. *Eur Psychiatry,* 22, 188–194.

Koenig, H.G. (2001). Religion and medicine II: Religion, mental health, and related behaviors. *Intl J Psychiatr Med,* 31, 97–109.

Lizardi, D., Dervic, K., Grunebaum, M.F., Burke, A.K., Mann, J.J., & Oquendo, A.A. (2008). The role of moral objections to suicide in the assessment of suicidal patients. *J Psychiatr Res,* 42, 815–821.

Malone, K.M., Oquendo, M.A., Haas, G.L., Ellis, S.P., Li, S., & Mann, J.J. (2000). Protective factors against suicidal acts in major depression: Reasons for living. *Am J Psychiatr,* 157, 1084–1088.

Moreira-Almeida, A., Neto, F.L., & Koenig, H.G. (2006). Religiousness and mental health: A review. *Rev Bras Psiquiatr,* 28, 242–250.

Nonnemaker, J.M., McNeely, C.A., & Blum, R.W. (2003). Public and private domains of religiosity and adolescent health risk behaviors: Evidence from the National Longitudinal Study of Adolescent Health. *Soc Sci Med,* 57, 2049–2054.

O'Mahony, S., Goulet, J., Kornblith, A., Abbatiello, G., Clarke, B., Kless-Siegel, S., Breitbart, W., & Payne, R. (2005). Desire for hastened death, cancer pain and depression: Report of a longitudinal observational study. *J Pain Symptom Manage,* 29, 446–457.

O'Neill, C., Feenan, D., Hughes, C., & McAlister, D.A. (2003). Physician and family-assisted suicide: Results from a study of public attitudes in Britain. *Soc Sci Med,* 57, 721–731.

Rasic, D.T., Belik, S.-L., Elias, B., Katz, L.Y., Enns, M., Sareen, J., & Swampy Cree Suicide Prevention Team. (2009). Spirituality, religion and suicidal behavior in a nationally representative. *J Affective Disorders,* 114, 32–40.

Rew, L., Thomas, N., Horner, S.D., Resnick, M., & Beuhring, T. (2001). Correlates of recent suicide attempts in a triethnic group of adolescents. *J Nurs Scholarsh,* 33, 361–367.

Thompson, A., & Taylor, N. (Eds.). (2006). *Hamlet: The Texts of 1603 and 1623*. The Arden Shakespeare, third ser. Vol. 2. London: Arden.

Viederman, M., & Perry, S.W. (1980). Use of a psychodynamic life narrative in the treatment of depression in the physically ill. *Gen Hosp Psychiatry*, 2, 177–185.

Walker, R.L., & Bishop, S. (2005). Examining a model of the relation between religiosity and suicidal ideation in a sample of African American and White college students. *Suicide Life Threat Behav*, 35, 630–639.

6 Models of Care

> Life can only be understood backwards; but it must be lived forwards.
>
> **Soren Kierkegaard**

In the preceding chapters, we have seen how the existential concerns of depressed individuals make it important to take their spiritual lives into account. But how feasible is it to simultaneously attend to body, mind, and soul, given the specialized ways in which mental health and spiritual professionals currently practice? In this chapter, I consider secular and faith-based models for integrating spiritual and emotional care for depression. I then consider the limitations of these models as challenging opportunities for improvement.

Care in Secular Settings

Psychiatry neglected religion for years after Freud attacked it as immature wish-fulfillment. However, several developments in the last quarter century have led to greater recognition of the positive contributions of spirituality in patients' lives. Palliative medicine, which has long valued spiritual care, and Alcoholics Anonymous, which advocates the Twelve Steps as a spiritual approach, have each grown in acceptance and influence. Researchers such as David Larson and Harold Koenig have reported studies, epidemiologic at first, on the associations between health outcomes and religiousness/spirituality. This literature has now grown to include studies of intrinsic versus extrinsic religiosity and religious coping and descriptions of spiritually oriented psychotherapy. Mindfulness, originally limited to Buddhist practitioners, is becoming an accepted tool for use in depression, including by secular therapists.[*] National meetings sponsored by organizations such as the Templeton Foundation, The Benson Henry Institute for Mind Body Medicine, and the Southern Medical Association have brought clinicians, chaplains, and other clergy together around issues of common concern, such as the provision of spiritual care in medical environments (e.g., at the end of life) or to individuals struggling with suicide. The Joint Commission now mandates that member institutions provide spiritual assessment and access to spiritual care, and that substance abuse treatment programs include a spiritual assessment of each patient. And a number of insurers ask participating providers whether they have expertise in "Christian therapy."

---

[*] Segal (2002).

What should an individual expect from a mental health professional working in secular settings? It seems reasonable to expect some basic form of spiritual assessment (for example, listening for what is centrally important to the patient, and asking screening questions such as, "Are you a spiritual or religious person?" or "What gives you peace?"*). This basic information can serve as a basis for further exploration and can help with treatment and referral for spiritual needs and distress that does not assume or encourage a particular world view. For example, an atheist patient seeing a Hindu therapist (or vice versa) could expect to have his spiritual concerns addressed as they bear on his presenting problem, even perhaps from within his world view (option three, as described in Chapter 4). He and the therapist might even explore these from within a shared world view (option four), if the patient coincidentally discovers that the therapist shares his world view (or asks) and the therapist decides it is clinically and ethically appropriate to disclose this information. The operative question, of course, in deciding whether to disclose is whether the benefit to the patient of using a shared understanding is worth the risk of influencing the patient by the perceived expectations of the therapist that might accompany this disclosure. Potential therapists of patients who seek out a therapist who shares their world view need to ask themselves the same question.

---

* Josephson and Peteet (2007).

While in theory an individual practitioner has considerable opportunity to practice integrated care within a secular setting, in practice he may encounter limitations. It can be difficult to find clergy within the institution to whom he can refer, and even more difficult to find those who are interested and/or experienced in working with patients suffering from mental illness. Other medical or mental health clinicians on the team may regard the patient's spirituality as off limits, irrelevant, or only discussable as a form of coping, or of "making meaning"—a conception which flattens it, deprives it of nuance and power, and leaves it with little to say about what life is or should be like.

Care in Faith-Based Settings

Faith-based organizations support the delivery of mental health services in several formats. These include through local religious congregations, networking and advocacy groups, national organizations that provide mission-driven social services, and groups that deliver faith-based mental health services but are not connected to a local or national religious group.[*] Yet some[†] have argued that forces such as historical tensions traceable at least to Freud, and the ascendancy of biological psychiatry have led Christian counselors and psychiatric practitioners to compartmentalize the insights of both traditions, so that spiritually and

---

[*] Koenig (2005).

[†] Blazer (1998).

emotionally integrated care is actually the exception rather than the rule. Consider some of the issues at stake in the provision of integrated care by pastors, pastoral counselors and therapists, spiritual directors, and faith-based communities.

Many pastors are frontline resources for help with both emotional and spiritual problems.[*,†] A survey by Ali et al.[‡] found that Muslim imams in the United States often deal with psychosocial needs, although they have limited formal training in counseling. A study of 99 clergy of black churches in a metropolitan area found that respondents averaged more than six hours of counseling work weekly.[§] These pastors often addressed serious problems similar to those seen by secular mental health professionals. Many observed and addressed severe mental illness and substance abuse in their congregations, and a number reported having and maintaining specialized education for their counseling work, which they described as including both spiritual and psychological dimensions. Most readily exchanged referrals with mental health professionals. However, pastors of immigrant, rural, and fundamentalist congregations sometimes fail members by applying spiritual approaches to mental illnesses, innocent of a psychological understanding of the illness—for example, by attempting to exorcise a bipolar patient instead of (rather than

---

[*] Taylor et al. (2000).

[†] Weaver (1995).

[‡] Ali et al. (2005).

[§] Young et al. (2003).

along with) encouraging him to take his mood stabilizers. Such pastors can also unintentionally risk intense transference reactions to their offers of intimate spiritual support when counseling trauma survivors or borderline individuals.

Pastors often refer to in-house or outside counselors of the same faith. Psychotherapy in a Christian or Muslim counseling center may be little different from that in a secular context. But help integrating spiritual and emotional concerns within the context of a particular faith is a common expectation of both patients and therapists in such a setting, within either the patient's (option three) or a shared world view (option four).

A pastoral counselor who is in a position of spiritual authority typically adopts a different role from that of a therapist—actively helping the individual to apply the teachings and resources of his faith to his emotional struggles. By inviting the individual to embrace a religious ideal, practice, or relationship, such a counselor (whether a pastor, pastoral assistant, or small group leader) is leading with a spiritual rather than with a psychological insight, even though he may draw on psychological knowledge to help the individual to better understand and address his resistance to making use of it. (An example might be questioning a person who says God is love, and assumes that God loves others, but has difficulty feeling loved by God.)

Pastoral therapists or counselors working in a faith-based setting may be subject to a number of limitations. Unless screened by experienced professionals, individuals whom they agree to see may need medication or intensive psychiatric treatment. Many faith-based organizations lack organic relationships with psychiatric practitioners or facilities that could facilitate referral for consultation, comanagement, and treatment. Individuals hoping to use their health insurance to pay for care may be unable to do so because of licensure or other reasons. At the same time, small churches may be unable to support a pastoral counselor without a mechanism for collecting fees, which also involves keeping records and managing risk.[*] Individuals may not want other members of their congregation to see them visiting a pastoral counselor for emotional problems. Unless clearly recognized and addressed, these problems can perpetuate troubling ambiguity about whether to think of pastoral counseling as a spiritual ministry of one's church, or as a service offered by a mental health provider.

Spiritual directors are trained individuals who often practice independently of churches or similar faith-based organizations, may expect a fee, and offer a spiritual approach directed not to resolving emotional problems such as depression per se, but to enhancing the individual's relationship with God.[†] This focus for the work makes clearer the nature of the relationship, but boundary issues can arise if the director is one's pastor or a member of one's congregation. Some individuals engage in both

---

[*] Griffith and Young (1987).
[†] Benner (2005).

spiritual direction and psychotherapy, at times concurrently, but if communication between director and therapist does not take place, a director may be unaware of character- or trauma-based transference problems influencing the work, or may be suggesting spiritual exercises similar to those the therapist has attempted. Spiritual directors may or may not have training in psychodynamic principles such as transference, splitting, and the repetition compulsion.

Beyond faith-based individual counseling, there are many ways that worshipping communities can help to ameliorate vulnerabilities to depression and address depressive concerns. A congregation can provide social support that is not primarily spiritual.[*,†,‡,§] The meta-narrative of a spiritual tradition can ground one's identity in life-changing ways; consider the examples of Malcolm X or Martin Luther King. Inventorying the ways that one is broken, confessing these, and claiming forgiveness can heal deep resentments against the self and others, providing a basis for hope. Sharing spiritual practices such as prayer, meditation, and service can help individuals maintain their sense of meaning and purpose. (Consider the best seller, *The Purpose Driven Life*.) Coming to experience God as for, rather than against one (in Pargament's terms, engaging in positive religious

---

[*] McRea (1998).
[†] Carter-Edwards et al. (2006).
[‡] Demark-Wahnfried et al. (2000).
[§] Walls and Zarit (1991).

coping), can change one's outlook on the self, on authority, and on life. And trusting God (or a power greater than oneself, in the terms of AA) with one's life can allow a person to let go of flawed, unrealistic, addictive, or selfish strategies for achieving happiness. The theologian Paul Tillich referred to this outcome as being clear that one's ultimate concern is placed in an object that is in fact ultimate (and not, for example, in power, prestige, or possessions).

> A 32-year-old mother presented with tearfulness, self-deprecating thoughts, feelings of being burdened if not overwhelmed, and chronic preoccupation with her weight. She described being increasingly frustrated by feeling that no one understood her emotional struggles. Having experienced a sense of forgiveness through her faith, she was particularly disappointed that her church's preaching instead seemed to be admonishing her.
>
> She recalled studying and competing hard from an early age, to please a critical mother. In high school she became anorexic and required outpatient treatment. She felt happy for a time as a new Christian in a college ministry, but plans for seminary lapsed because she felt unable to live up to her expectations of what a pastor or chaplain should be like.
>
> The therapist's formulation was that perfectionistic traits predisposed her to depression and isolation. Her faith was both a resource for forgiveness, but also an exacerbating factor when she found church authorities demanding and judgmental.
>
> When at her therapist's encouragement she spoke with one of her pastors, she felt relief at being heard and prayed for. She benefitted even more from finding another congregation where discussion of and prayer for life issues, primarily in small group settings, was a larger part of the church's life.

Without advising her which church to choose, her therapist used his knowledge of differences among churches, and of her emotional strengths and vulnerabilities, to help her think through what kinds of worship experiences and settings would best enhance her relationship with God.

Some religious communities identify depression as a sin and evidence of lack of faith, or even of a demonic spirit (the Spirit of Depression). Others, though they acknowledge a role for counseling, still see depression as spiritual at its core.[*,†] This can of course oversimplify the nature of serious depression, risk inducing shame and worsening guilt, and discount the painful nature of spiritual struggles such as the dark night of the soul. On the other hand, skilled practitioners can use theological categories to encourage individuals to confront rather than to accept or indulge depression, and to draw on spiritual resources in seeking liberation from its oppressive power. Even conservative Christians increasingly view psychiatric resources such as antidepressant medication (if perhaps less so psychotherapy) as valued weapons in this struggle.[‡,§]

In large areas of the developing world such as Africa, traditional and faith healers see and manage most mental health problems. A recent study of faith healers in a Nairobi slum found

---

[*] Lahaye (1996).
[†] Sutton and Hennigan (2001).
[‡] Biebel and Koenig (2004).
[§] Hall (2009).

that depression was the disorder they diagnosed most often.[*] A majority favored the creation of programs for sharing ideas with practitioners of Western-style medicine.

How often are faith-based therapeutic (and at times anti-therapeutic) influences integrated with an understanding of the psychiatric needs of depressed individuals? This seems to vary greatly, but a number of interesting models have begun to emerge. Catholics have recognized the potential of Ignatian spiritual exercises for fostering personal emotional growth[†] and have at times incorporated psychologists in assessing and providing both direct and indirect care for parishioners' needs.[‡] Tyler et al.[§] have suggested a role "resource collaborator" for such situations. Faith-based group programs such as Living Waters[¶] focus on helping individuals to face their personal "brokenness" in areas such as trauma and sexual addiction, and find healing before God.

How effective are faith-based models of integrated care and collaboration? Research into this question is in its infancy. There is some evidence that pastoral care[**] and lay faith-based counseling

---

[*] Ndetei (2008).
[†] Meissner (1999).
[‡] Benes et al. (2000).
[§] Tyler et al. (1983).
[¶] Desert Stream Ministries (2010).
[**] Baker (2000).

can have positive mental health outcomes,[*] but studies looking both at mental health and spiritual outcomes are lacking.

Future Challenges

Koenig[†] has outlined many of the barriers to research and implementation of integrated care, such as the paucity of funding, negative attitudes toward religion, inadequate training, overregulation, and the stigma of mental illness. Several additional obstacles remain at the level of the individual clinician: One is the human tendency of caregivers, whether mental health or spiritual, to rely on a few paradigms of choice, whether biological, psychodynamic, behavioral, or existential. Another is the propensity of professional training, peers, and the pharmaceutical industry to reinforce continued reliance on such paradigms. A third is the difficulty that scientifically oriented clinicians often have in embracing a dimension of experience that they cannot fully understand. Yet another is the reluctance of many religious individuals (as well as some clergy) to trust clinicians with spiritual questions. Perhaps the most challenging is the need for therapists of depressed individuals to face and resolve their own concerns in the areas of identity, hope, purpose, morality, connection, and relationship to ultimate authority, or God.

---

[*] Toh et al. (1997).

[†] Koenig (2005, pp. 243–254).

In this chapter, I have attempted to describe the strengths and limitations of basic models currently in use in the hope that they will suggest possible improvements. Consider a few possibilities: A partnership between a secular hospital and local congregations could meet the needs of church-based counselors for psychiatric screening and backup, while offering the hospital support in achieving its goals of more comprehensive, community-based treatment and education. Congregations with programs such as Living Waters that encourage personal transformation through spiritual means may benefit from using psychiatric consultation or supervision to screen troubled (for example, recently suicidal) individuals, so as to ensure they are also engaged in concurrent, coordinated mental health treatment. Stronger connections between spiritual directors or meditation leaders and clinicians could enhance communication about shared cases and help clinicians to recognize their limits in dealing with areas unfamiliar to them and to make more effective referrals.

Research on the outcomes of such models could incorporate measures of existential and spiritual as well emotional well-being. Studies of their cost-effectiveness may need to track treatment that is directed toward existential or spiritual problems, such as using the DSM-IV V Code for Religious or Spiritual Problem.

Finally, with respect to education, sharing clinical experiences both informally (e.g., in case conferences) and in venues such as interdisciplinary rounds and medical school, residency, and graduate-level courses continue to be important means of demonstrating the practical implications of connections among body, mind, and soul.

To summarize, in this chapter we have examined secular and faith-based models for integrating spiritual and emotional care, highlighting the potential and the limitations of each. We have then briefly noted the barriers to providing integrated care and the challenges that these present for needed collaboration in the areas of improved care, service research, and mutual learning.

References

Ali, O.M., Milstein, G., & Marzuk, P.M. (2005). The Imam's role in meeting the counseling needs of Muslim communities in the United States, *Psychiatric Serv,* 56, 202–205.

Baker, D. (2000). The investigation of pastoral care interventions as a treatment for depression among continuing care retirement community residents. *J Religious Gerontology,* 12, 63–85.

Benes, K.M., Walsh, J.M., McMinn, M.R., Dominguez, A.W., & Aikins, D.C. (2000). Psychology and the church: An exemplar of psychologist-clergy collaboration. *Professional Psychology: Research and Practice,* 31, 515–520.

Benner, D. (2005). Intensive soul care: Integrating psychotherapy and spiritual direction. In L. Sperry & E. Shafranske (Eds.), *Spiritually Oriented Psychotherapy.* Washington, DC: American Psychological Association, pp. 287–306.

Biebel, D., & Koenig, H.G. (2004). *New Light on Depression: Help, Hope and Answers for the Depressed and Those Who Love Them.* Grand Rapids, MI: Zondervan.

Blazer, D.G. (1998). *Freud Versus God: How Psychiatry Lost Its Soul and Christianity Lost Its Mind.* Downers Grove, IL: InterVarsity Press.

Carter-Edwards, L., Jallah, Y.B., Goldmond, M.V., Roberson, J.T., & Hoyo, C. (2006). Key attributes of health ministries in African American churches: An exploratory survey. *N C Med, J,* 67, 345–350.

Demark-Wahnefried, W., McClelland, J.W., Jackson, B., Campbell, M.K., Cowan, A., Hoben, K., & Rimer, B.K. (2000). Partnering with African American churches to achieve better health: Lessons learned during the Black Churches United for Better Health 5 a day project. *J Cancer Educ,* 15, 164–167.

Desert Stream Ministries. (2010). Living Waters. http://desertstream.org/Groups/1000040175/Desert_Stream_Ministries/Who_We_Are/Affiliated_Programs/Living_Waters/Living_Waters.aspx. Accessed January 24, 2010.

Griffith, E.E., & Young, J.L. (1987). Pastoral counseling and the concept of malpractice. *Bull Am Acad Psychiatry Law,* 15, 257–265.

Hall, D.P. (2009). *Breaking Through Depression: A Biblical and Medical Approach to Emotional Wholeness.* Eugene, OR: Harvest House Publishers.

Josephson, A.M., & Peteet, J.R. (2007). Talking with patients about spirituality and worldview: Practical interviewing techniques and strategies. *Psychiatr Clin N Am,* 30, 181–197.

Koenig, H.G. (2005). *Faith and Mental Health: Religious Resources for Healing.* West Conshohocken, PA: Templeton Foundation Press.

Lahaye, T. (1996). *How to Win Over Depression.* Grand Rapids, MI: Zondervan.

McRae, M.B., Carey, P.M., & Anderson-Scott, R. (1998). Black churches as therapeutic systems: A group process perspective. *Health Educ Behav,* 25, 778–789.

Meissner, W.W. (1999). *To the Greater Glory: A Psychological Study of Ignatian Spirituality.* Milwaukee, WI: Marquette University Press.

Ndetei, David. (2008). Personal communication, October 6, 2008.

Segal, Z.V., Williams, J.M.G., & Teasdale, J.D. (2002). *Mindfulness-Based Cognitive Therapy for Depression: A New Approach to Preventing Relapse.* New York: Guilford Press.

Sutton, M., Hennigan, B. (2001). *Conquering Depression.* Nashville, TN: Broadman and Holman, Publishers.

Taylor, R.J., Ellison, C.G., Chatters, L.M., Levin, J.S., & Lincoln, K.D. (2000). Mental health services in faith communities: The role of clergy in black churches. *Soc Work,* 45, 73–87.

Toh, Y.T., & Tan, S.Y. (1997). The effectiveness of church-based lay counselors: A controlled outcome study. *J Psychology Christianity,* 16, 260–267.

Tyler, F.B., Pargament, K.I., & Gatz, M. (1983). The resource collaborator role: A model for interactions involving psychologists. *American Psychologist,* 38, 388–398.

Walls, C.T., & Zarit, S.H. (1991). Informal support from black churches and the well-being of elderly blacks. *Gerontologist,* 31, 490–495.

Weaver, A.J. (1995). Has there been a failure to prepare and support parish-based clergy in their role as frontline community mental health workers? A review. *J Pastoral Care,* 49, 129–147.

Young, J.L., Griffith, E.E., & Williams, D.R. (2003). The integral role of pastoral counseling by African American clergy in community mental health. *Psychiatr Serv,* 54, 688–692.

7 The Brain, Depression, and Spirituality

> The relationship between affective and moral sensibility is complex.
>
> **Peter Kramer,** *Listening to Prozac*

A growing number of individuals understand depression as a "chemical imbalance" that requires medication. To others, depression is a disorder that is spiritual at its core. Owing to this divergence of perspective, many assume that biological and spiritual approaches are incompatible. In this chapter we consider (1) the neurobiology of mood and of spirituality; (2) biological treatments for depression; (3) the philosophical and moral implications of biology for approaching conditions associated with depressed mood; and (4) a basis for an integrated perspective.

Neurobiology

Emotion has long been associated with the brain's limbic–frontal circuits. Specifically, findings from both animal and human lesion studies, as well as from functional neuroimaging, suggest that emotion is mediated by two neural systems.* The first, located in the amygdala (associated with goal-directed behavior and anxiety), ventral striatum (associated with reward), insula and ventral regions of the anterior cingulate gyrus, and prefrontal cortex, appears to generate emotion in response to a stimulus. The second, located in the hippocampus (associated with memory) and dorsal regions of anterior cingulate gyrus and prefrontal cortex, appears to regulate the organism's affective state. Activity in the left prefrontal cortex as compared with the right correlates with positive emotion.† Stress-related activation of the amygdala leads in turn to stimulation of the hypothalamic–pituitary–adrenal axis and hippocampus, involving corticotropin-releasing factor (CRF), glucocorticoids, and brain-derived neurotrophic factor. Other limbic structures such as the nucleus accumbens, amygdala, and certain hypothalamic nuclei are involved with motivation, arousal, sleeping, eating, energy level, circadian rhythm, and responses to aversive and rewarding stimuli, which can all become abnormal in depressed individuals.‡

Studies of brain functioning in depression focused initially on the actions of antidepressants in regulating the functional availability of monoamine neurotransmitters such as serotonin, norepinephrine, and dopamine. However, more recently, their influence on the structure of the hippocampus and amygdala of

---

* Phillips et al. (2003).

† Davidson (2001).

‡ Nestler et al. (2002).

depressed individuals has suggested that they may have important neuroprotective functions.[*,†] Both amygdala hypertrophy and elevated and sustained amygdala activity in response to aversive stimuli are common in unipolar depression. All classes of antidepressants currently on the market promote neurogenesis in the dentate gyrus, perhaps mediated by brain-derived neurotropic factor (BDNF).

Investigators have also focused attention on the genetic vulnerability of depressed individuals to dysregulation of the hypothalamic–pituitary–adrenal axis. Growing evidence suggests that early life trauma such as physical or sexual abuse may be more likely to result in long-lasting changes in pituitary-mediated stress response and an increased risk of depression.[‡] Antidepressants reverse cortisol-induced downregulation of BDNF in the hippocampus.

Research into the neurobiology of spirituality has also implicated the limbic system stress response and neurotransmitter function. For example, neuroimaging of meditators has shown activation of the prefrontal cortex, activation of the thalamus and the inhibitory thalamic reticular nucleus, and a resultant functional inactivation of the parietal lobe.[§] Both Buddhist

---

[*] McEwen and Olie (2005).
[†] Young et al. (2002).
[‡] Nemeroff and Vale (2005).
[§] Mohandas (2008).

meditators[*] and Carmelite nuns show increased activity of the left prefrontal cortex, associated with the experience of positive emotions.[†] Pollard's[‡] comprehensive review of the effects of meditation notes a number of effects on stress responsiveness. And Nilsson et al.[§] have correlated serotonin receptor polymorphism with measures of the character traits of self-transcendence and spiritual acceptance.

Biological Treatments

Electroconvulsive therapy (ECT), first used in 1937, became widespread in the treatment of severe depression in the 1940s and 1950s. Antidepressant drug treatment began in 1952, when antituberculous drugs that inhibited the enzyme monoamine oxidase were observed to benefit some depressed individuals. Many drugs acting on neurotransmitters in other ways have since been approved for the treatment of major depression, including the tricyclics, the selective serotonin reuptake inhibitors (SSRIs), and the serotonin norepinephrine reuptake inhibitors (SNRIs). Meta-analyses of studies of antidepressant efficacy such as that performed by Kirsch et al.[¶] have found drug treatment better than placebo at conventional levels of statistical significance only

---

[*] Davidson and Harrington (2002, p. 17).
[†] Beauregard and Paquette (2006).
[‡] Pollard (2004).
[§] Nilsson et al. (2007).
[¶] Kirsch et al. (2008).

at the upper end of the severely depressed category, owing to the lack of efficacy of placebo at this level. For individuals in this category, evidence has also been accumulating for the effectiveness of other physical treatments including, in addition to ECT, vagal nerve stimulation, repetitive transcranial magnetic stimulation, and deep brain stimulation.

Implications of Biology

The implications of these scientific advances are both clinical and philosophical.

Medication and other biological interventions emerged as accepted treatments for the most severe forms of depression in a time when a psychodynamic model was dominant, and by the 1970s had become the standard of care.[*] Today, the SSRIs are among the most widely prescribed medications in developed countries. The widespread use of SSRIs and other antidepressants for conditions other than depression (notably anxiety) reflects a shift away from thinking about them as specific remedies for discrete and disabling disorders (as insulin is for diabetes, or penicillin for pneumococcal pneumonia) to thinking of them as modulators of symptoms, or as potential enhancers of normal capacities and personality.[†,‡] Meanwhile, agents classified

---

[*] Klerman (1990).

[†] Kramer (1993).

[‡] Tang et al. (2009).

as atypical antipsychotics, such as apiperazole, are also being approved for the treatment of depression.

While considerable research now focuses on the genetic makeup of individuals most likely to benefit from antidepressants, most clinicians continue to prescribe those agents that seem most likely to remediate target symptoms (for example, emotional reactivity, anergia, or insomnia). However, mental health professionals differ considerably, for reasons of philosophy and training, in their threshold for prescribing a medication before exploring the patient's experience and trying other approaches.

The philosophical and sociocultural implications of a biological perspective can perhaps be seen most clearly in historical context. The British scientist C.P. Snow, referring to the impact of Cartesian dualism that developed in the Enlightenment, famously contrasted in a 1959 lecture the "two cultures" of the sciences and the humanities, as they embody objective and subjective ways of knowing, respectively.[*] More recently, Tanya Luhrmann, an anthropologist and daughter of a psychiatrist, has explored the tension between these perspectives for a specialty that attempts to encompass both the inner and the bodily experience of the person. She writes in her book *Of Two Minds: The Growing Disorder in American Psychiatry*[†]:

> These two ideals embody different moral sensibilities, different fundamental commitments, different bottom lines. In some ways

---

[*] Snow (1959/1998).

[†] Luhrmann (2000).

the differences are subtle; in others they are sharp and striking. The differences become part of the way the young psychiatrist imagines himself with patients, the way he comes to empathize with patients, and, ultimately, the way he comes to regard his patients as moral beings. (p. 158)

The differences in psychiatrists' fundamental commitments are sharpest when those with a biological perspective (like some of their predecessors with strong psychoanalytic commitments) offer reductionistic explanations and promote simplistic solutions. The provocative observations of Horwitz and Wakefield[*] in *The Loss of Sadness: How Psychiatry Transformed Normal Sorrow into Depressive Disorder* build on those of Philip Rieff in his 1965 book *The Triumph of the Therapeutic,* in which he argued that our society is only too ready to see human problems in therapeutic or medical terms. Familiar critiques of direct-to-consumer and other forms of marketing by pharmaceutical companies proceed along the same lines.

Peter Kramer in his landmark work *Listening to Prozac*[†] pursues further ethical questions raised by what he terms "cosmetic psychopharmacology." If a serotonin reuptake inhibitor is helpful with mild symptoms, is it important whether these meet criteria for a mental disorder? What are the consequences of using such medications to alter personality, enhancing capacities to make one "better than well"? What if they temper one's sensitivity to

---

[*] Horwitz and Wakefield (2007).

[†] Kramer (1993).

one's own suffering and that of others, depriving the individual of what he could otherwise learn, or numbing him to ills in society that should grieve him?

Attempts to answers these questions leads to more basic philosophical questions that have a spiritual dimension: (1) what is the purpose of medicine and therefore the role of the physician, and (2) how can one weigh the costs and benefits of sensitivity to suffering?

Psychopharmacological liberals believe that physicians should use medical technology to enhance functioning, whereas conservatives question whether this as a legitimate extension of the physician's traditional role to treat the sick.[*] As patients increasingly ask their physicians to prescribe medications that they may have found through direct advertizing, physicians find themselves challenged to examine their basic commitments, whether to accommodate the patient's choice, or to insist on doing what they believe is good for the patient. Their world views influence how they define and pursue this good.[†,‡]

Concerns about the potential benefits of sensitivity to suffering in oneself and others also may also be spiritually based. Taking medication to relieve distress associated with ordinary living can seem like "playing God," rather than relying on Him. Spiritually oriented individuals may also feel that taking

---

[*] Chatterjee (2006).

[†] Bishop et al. (2007).

[‡] Curlin et al. (2007).

medication deprives them of other benefits such as learning to be grateful, holy, or aware of the needs of others. Some, more puritanically oriented individuals may feel that taking medication is escapist, in the same way that some members of Alcoholics Anonymous Twelve Step view taking pills as equivalent to "chewing booze." And patients who, when depressed, experience God as judgmental may feel that they deserve to suffer.[*]

An Integrated Perspective

Advances in neurobiology and psychopharmacology have generated understandable enthusiasm for biological solutions to vexing human problems, raising both practical and theoretical questions about how to combine them with other ways of understanding and approaching depression. Consider four possible foundations for an integrated perspective, which sees the mind and brain as reflecting a single reality:

First, both mood states and spiritual experience have distinct but overlapping brain correlates, as discussed above. It is therefore misleading to assume that biological, psychological, or spiritual dimensions of the self are immiscible.[†]

Second, there is evidence that psychotherapy and spiritual practice as well as medication produce detectable changes in

---

[*] Peteet (2006).

[†] Damasio (2005).

the brain.[*,†] Biological and these other interventions are equally "real" in their effects.

Third, as Blazer[‡] has shown in his book *The Age of Melancholy: "Major Depression" and Its Social Origins,* depression occurs in a social context that also has a spiritual dimension. Some societies appear to foster guilt and depression, whereas others protect against it, often by helping individuals to preserve their identity through a shared meta-narrative. Spiritual answers to existential questions are important even in conditions that have a biological component, such as major depression.

Fourth, evidence indicates that the best outcomes in the treatment of depression result from combining medication and psychotherapy.[§] Similar studies have not yet been performed to determine whether combining spiritual, psychotherapeutic, and biological interventions confers additional, demonstrable benefit.

We began this chapter by reviewing the neurobiology of mood and spirituality, noting areas of overlap. We then considered reasons for the growth of biological interventions for depression, as well as some of their far-reaching cultural and philosophical implications. Finally, we suggested four bases for an integrated perspective. Like the proverbial blind men examining an elephant, those of us who are impressed with

---

[*] Etkin et al. (2005).

[†] Lazar et al. (2005).

[‡] Blazer (2005).

[§] Rush and Thase (1999).

the power of biological, psychological, or spiritual interventions are naturally inclined to interpret the whole from our particular points of view. In preceding chapters, we have emphasized the need to tailor interventions to the individual's particular needs. This task will be made easier if we can remember that the suffering of depressed individuals always has a social and a spiritual context, as well as a physical substrate in the brain.

References

Beauregard, M., & Paquette, V. (2006). Neural correlates of a mystical experience in Carmelite nuns. *Neuroscience Letters,* 405, 186–190.

Bishop, L., Josephson, A., Thielman, S., & Peteet, J. (2007). Neutrality, autonomy and mental health: A closer look. *Bull Menninger Clin,* 71, 164–178.

Blazer, D.G. (2005). *The Age of Melancholy: "Major Depression" and Its Social Origins.* New York: Routledge.

Chatterjee, A. (2006). The promise and predicament of cosmetic neurology. *J Med Ethics,* 32, 110–113.

Curlin, F.A., Lawrence, R.E., Chin, M.A., & Lantos, J.D. (2007). Religion, conscience and controversial clinical practices. *New Engl J Med,* 365, 593–600.

Damasio, A. (2005). *Descartes' Error: Emotion, Reason and the Human Brain* (10th ed.). New York: Penguin Books.

Davidson, R.J. (2001). Toward a biology of personality and emotion. *NY Acad Sci,* 935, 191–207.

Davidson, R.J., & Harrington, A. (Eds.). (2002). *Visions of Compassion: Western Scientists and Tibetan Buddhists Examine Human Nature.* New York: Oxford University Press.

Etkin, A., Pittenger, C., Polan, H.J., & Kandel, E.R. (2005). Toward a neurobiology of psychotherapy: Basic science and clinical applications. *J Neuropsychiatry Clin Neurosci,* 17, 145–158.

Horwitz, A.V., & Wakefield, J.C. (2007). *The Loss of Sadness: How Psychiatry Transformed Normal Sorrow Into Depressive Disorder.* New York: Oxford University Press.

Kirsch, I., Deacon, B.J., Huedo-Medina, T.B., Scoboria, A., Moore, T.J., & Johnson, B.T. (2008). Initial severity and antidepressant drug benefits: A meta-analysis of data submitted to the Food and Drug Administration. *PLoS Med* 5(2): e45. doi:10.1371/journal.pmed.0050045.

Klerman, G.L. (1990). The psychiatric patient's right to effective treatment: Implications of Osheroff v. Chestnut Lodge. *Am J Psychiatry,* 147, 409–418.

Kramer, P. (1993). *Listening to Prozac.* New York: Viking Press.

Lazar, S.W., Kerr, C.E., Wasserman, R.H., Gray, J.R., Greve, D.N., Treadway, M.T., McGarvey, M., Quinn, B.T., Dusek, J.A., Benson, H., Rauch, S.L., Moore, C.I., & Fischl B. (2005). Meditation experience is associated with increased cortical thickness. *Euroreport,* 16, 1893–1897.

Luhrmann, T.M. (2000). *Of Two Minds: The Growing Disorder in American Psychiatry.* New York: Alfred A. Knopf.

McEwen, B.S., & Olie, J. (2005). Neurobiology of mood, anxiety and emotions as revealed by studies of a unique antidepressant: Tianaptine. *Molecular Psychiatry,* 10, 525–537.

Mohandas, E. (2008). Neurobiology of spirituality. *Mental Health Spirituality Mind,* 6, 63–80.

Nemeroff, C.B., & Vale, W.W. (2005). The neurobiology of depression: Inroads to treatment and new drug discovery. *J Clin Psychiatry,* 66, 5–13 (Supplement).

Nestler, E., Barrot, M., DiLeone, R., Eisch, A., Gold, A., & Monteggia, L. (2002). Neurobiology of depression. *Neuron,* 34, 13–25.

Nilsson, K.W., Damberg, M., Öhrvik, J., Leppert, J., Lindström, L., Anckarsäter, H., & Oreland, L. (2007). Genes encoding for AP-2β and the serotonin transporter are associated with the personality character spiritual acceptance. *Neuroscience Letters,* 411, 233–237.

Peteet, J.R. (2006). Disease as punishment. *South Med J,* 99, 434–435.

Phillips, M.L., Drevets, W.C., Rauch, S.L., & Lane, R. (2003). Neurobiology of emotion perception I: The neural basis of normal emotion perception. *Biological Psychiatry,* 54, 504–514.

Pollard, I. (2004). Meditation and brain function: A review. *Eubios J Asian International Bioethics,* 14, 28–34.

Rush, A.J., & Thase, M.E. (1999). Psychotherapies for depressive disorders. In M. Maj & N. Sartorius (Eds.), *World Psychiatric Association Series on Evidence and Practice in Psychiatry*, Vol. 1. Depressive Disorders. Chichester, England: John Wiley, pp. 161–206.

Snow, C.P. (1959/1998). *The Two Cultures.* Cambridge, UK: Cambridge University Press.

Tang, T.G., DeRubeis, R.J., Hollon, S.D., Amsterdam, J., Shelton, R., & Schalet, S.D. (2009). Personality change during depression treatment. *Arch Gen Psychiatry,* 66, 1322–1330.

Young, L.T., Bakish, D., & Beaulieu, S. (2002). The neurobiology of treatment response to antidepressants and mood stabilizing medications. *J Psychiatry Neurosci,* 27, 260–265.

Index

Note: "f" indicates material in figures. "t" indicates material in tables. "n" indicates material in footnotes.

A

AA; *See* Alcoholics Anonymous
Abuse
    child; *See* Child abuse
    physical, 32, 81, 126, 187
    sexual, 56, 81, 132, 156, 158, 187
    spiritual direction and, 119
    treatment and memories of, 125
    verbal, 32, 124, 126
Acceptance, 17–18, 78, 131, 138, 188
Acceptance and commitment therapy (ACT), 6
Acedia, 88
ACT, 6
Adams, Jay, 46
Addiction, 49, 79, 98f; *See also* Twelve Step Programs
Adjustment disorder, 85–87, 98f, 102
Affect, 4, 152, 186; *See also* Emotions
African Americans, 40, 43, 173
Against Happiness (Wilson), 59
Age of Melancholy, The (Blazer), 34, 194
Agnostics, 12
Ainslie, G., 4–5
Akiskal, H.S., 72
Alcohol abuse, 60, 79, 88
Alcoholics Anonymous (AA)
    choices in, 114
    forgiveness in, 57
    identity in, 56, 120
    influence of, 170
    integrity in, 120
    medication and, 193
    misconceptions about, 136
    referrals to, 139
    spiritual maturity and, 60, 79–80
    trust in, 177
    "working the Program," 17, 80
Ali, O.M., 173
Altruism, 10
Amends, making, 18
American Psychiatric Association
    DSM; *See Diagnostic and Statistical Manual of Mental Disorders*
    on recovery, 2
Amygdala, 186–187
Anger
    over authority, 136
    Jewish tradition on, 44

self-sacrifice and, 131
over sexual abuse, 81, 132
suicide and, 160
treatment for, 132, 138
Angst, 87–89, 98f
Anhedonia, 3–4
Anorexia, 56, 60–61
Anticipation, 15
Antidepressants
for adjustment disorder, 86
amygdala and, 186–187
assessment prior to prescribing, 97
BDNF and, 187
Christians and, 178
efficacy of, 188–189
hippocampus and, 186–187
history of, 188
melancholy and, 74
neurotransmitters and, 186
prescribing of, 189–190
psychotherapeutic treatment and, ix
SNRIs, 188
spiritual direction and, 119
SRIs, 77, 78, 188
SSRIs, 188, 189
substance abuse and, 79
Antipsychotics, 74, 190
Antituberculous drugs, 188
Anxiety
in ACT, 6
in adjustment disorder, 85
angst and, 87–88
CBT for, 112
function of, 4
neurobiology of, 186
SSRIs for, 189
Apiperazole, 190
Approaches to the Mind (Havens), 8–9
Aristotle, xi
Art, 17, 159
Atheists, 12, 52–53, 57, 137–138
Authenticity, 7
Authority, relationships to
abuse and, 32, 54, 81, 132, 156

anger over, 136
betrayal in, 32
depression and, 36, 53, 121t
identity and, 130
IPT for, 19, 117, 121t, 123
morality and, 18
psychodynamic approach for, 121t, 123
spiritual direction for, 121t, 123
spirituality and, 14, 19–21, 121t, 123, 176–177
world view and, 14, 19, 137
Autonomy, 10, 19, 99, 137
Awareness
Buddhists on, 59
after dark night of the soul, 92
in MBCT, 113
of "soul-nourishing" activities, 115
in spiritual direction, 118
spirituality and, 58
substance abuse and, 89
Twelve Step Programs and, 20
Ayurvedic tradition, 51
Azhar, M.Z., 39

B

Barrigan, Cardinal, 34
BDNF, 187
Beck, A.T., 153
Beckett, Samuel, 52–53
Ben-Shahar, Tal D., 95
Benner, D.G., 119, 120
Benson Henry Institute for Mind Body Medicine, The, 170
Benzodiazepines, 88
Bergin, Richard, 10
Bible
on Elijah, 44
on Job, 44, 127
on King Saul's moods, 44
New Testament; *See* New Testament
Psalms, 44, 59

Biopsychosocial approach, 9
Bipolar disorder, 50, 75, 76, 98f, 173–174
Black church clergy, 173
Blazer, Dan, 34, 47, 194
Block, S.D., 83
Bonhoeffer, Dietrich, 89–90
Borderline personality disorder, 57, 159, 174
Born-again Christians, 46, 54
Boscaglia, N., 42
Brain-derived neurotropic factor (BDNF), 187
Breitbart, W., 16, 114
Broaden-and-build theory, 7
Buddha, 50
Buddhists
    on bipolar disorder, 50
    brain studies of, 187–188
    CBT and, 50, 112
    depression and, 38, 49–51, 53
    Four Noble Truths of, 15, 49–50
    on identity, 15
    MBCT and, 112
    meditation by, 17, 50
    on suffering, 59, 138
    suicide and, 20, 152, 154n
Bunyan, John, 46

C

Camus, Albert, 33, 52–53
Canadian Community Health Survey, 151
Caring, 18
Cassell, E.J., 83
"Cathected" activities, 4
Catholics
    brain studies of nuns, 188
    on depression, 49
    divorce and, 55
    Ignatian Exercises, 49, 118, 179
    Jesuits, 49
    sexual abuse by priest, 132

CBT; *See* Cognitive behavioral therapy
Celebration of Discipline (Foster), 48
Child abuse
    anger over, 81, 132
    authority and, 32, 54, 81, 132
    coping strategies for, 37
    guilt over, 35, 132
    hope and, 32, 54, 56, 81, 127
    insecurity after, 81, 132
    marriage to escape, 32, 126
    neurobiology of, 187
    reporting of, 81, 132
    self-sacrifice and, 132
    shame from, 81, 132
    spirituality and, 54, 56, 81, 127, 132
    stress and, 187
    suicide and, 32, 126–127, 158
    trauma from, 32, 81, 126, 158
    treatment and, 125
    trust after, 32, 56, 158
Christians; *See also* Jesus
    born-again, 46, 54
    Catholics; *See* Catholics
    CBT and, 38, 112
    depression and, 38, 45–49, 53
    Kierkegaard on, 89
    Protestants; *See* Protestants
    resources for, 174, 178
    on suffering, 138
    suicide and, 152
Chronic characterological depression, 76
Chronic fatigue syndrome, 35–36
Cigarette smoking, 79
Cingulate gyrus, 186
Cloninger, Robert, 17, 77–78
Cocaine, 60, 79
Cognition, 10
Cognitive behavioral therapy (CBT)
    for anxiety, 112
    for bipolar disorder, 98f
    for Buddhists, 50, 112
    for Christians, 38, 112
    emotions in, 5–6

goal of, 6
hope and, 121t, 122
for Jews, 112
mindfulness in, 6
for Muslims, 112
for perfectionists, 128, 133
religious, 38, 111–112, 136
resilience in, 6
resistance to, 144
self in, 133
for trauma, 133
world view and, 138
Cole, B., 120
Coleman, C.L., 40
Coles, Robert, 91
Commitments
and acceptance therapy, 6
altruistic, 60
faith and, 15
morality and, 18
postmodernism on, 22
relationships and, 7, 10
suicide and, 151, 152, 157, 162
Compassion, 13, 16, 45, 50, 93, 114–115
Competent to Counsel (Adams), 46
Confession, 18, 49
Conflict, 4, 52, 100–101, 117, 125
Conflict resolution workshops, 86
Control, 19, 73
Cooper, L.A., 43
Coping
Christian tradition on, 46–47
Multidimensional Measurement on, 13
Pargament on, 36, 90, 176–177
religious belief and, 39
strategies for, 37, 43, 152, 156
transformation and, 47
in Vaillant's models, 8
Corticotropin-releasing factor (CRF), 186
Courage, 5, 8, 10, 84, 95, 115
Courage to Be, The (Tillich), 16, 88

Coyne, J.C., 76
Crazy Busy (Hallowell), 34
CRF, 186
Cults, 54–55
Cultural beliefs, 11, 34, 82
Cunningham, J., 43
Cynicism, 16

D

Dalai Lama, 15
Dark night of the soul
adjustment disorder and, 87
awareness after, 92
compassion and, 93
depression and, 87, 93
description of, 45, 91–94
diagnosis of, 98f
discounting, 178
meditation during, 92
phases of, 92
prayer during, 92
relationship with God and, 61, 92–93
spiritual direction during, 48, 124
in transformation, 48
Dark Night of the Soul (John of the Cross), 45, 61, 91–92
Dark Night of the Soul, The (May), 48, 93
Darkness Visible (Styron), 72–73
DBT, 17–18, 78, 159
Death, 5, 23; *See also* Suicide
Deep brain stimulation, 189
Delusions, 58, 74, 75, 157
Demonic spirits, 178
Demoralization, 83–85, 98f, 124
Dentate gyrus, 187
Depression
vs. acedia, 88
in adjustment disorder, 85–87
Akiskal and McKinney on, 72
assessment of, 96–100
case formulation for, 100–105

vs. demoralization, 84
diagnosis of, 98f
dysthymia, 76–77, 127
humoral theory of, 74
major; *See* Major depression
melancholic features of, 73, 74
neurobiology of, 185–187
psychotic features of, 73
PTSD and, 80
recurrence of, 73
risk factors for, 73
sorrow and, 73, 94
stress diathesis model for, 74
symptoms of, 72
unhappiness and, 94–95
vulnerability to, 73
Dervic, K., 151, 160
Descartes, René, 21
Despair
acedia and, 88
demoralization and, 84, 124
grief and, 124
hope and, 16, 54
humanistic approaches for, 133
Kierkegaard on, 87
positive psychology for, 133
Psalm on, 44
trust and, 122
Determinism, 4
Diagnostic and Statistical Manual of Mental Disorders (DSM)
depressive personality in, 76
GAF, 8
on grief, 82, 84
Major Depressive Disorder in, 72
Outline for a Cultural Formulation in, 101
reliance on, 94
on Religious or Spiritual Problems, 96, 181
Dialectical behavioral therapy (DBT), 17–18, 78, 159
Dimensional perspective, 9
Disease perspective, 9

Divorce, 55
Donne, John, 35
Dopamine, 186
Drug abuse, 60, 79
DSM; *See Diagnostic and Statistical Manual of Mental Disorders*
Dualism, 21, 190
Dublin, 43
Durkheim, Emil, 33, 150
Dysthymia, 76–77, 127

E

ECT, 74, 154, 188
Ego, 3–4
Electroconvulsive therapy (ECT), 74, 154, 188
Elijah, 44
Elkins, D.N., 115
Emmer, C., 92
Emotions
in ACT, 6
in CBT, 5–6
cognition and, 10
conflict and, 4
forgiveness-promoting therapy for, 115
Four Noble Truths on, 49
Freud on, 3–4
function of, 3
Ignatian Exercises and, 179
in IPT, 6
libidinal drives/wishes and, 3–4
Muslims and, 52
neurobiology of, 185–188
pastoral counseling for, 173–175
in positive psychology, 7
in psychoanalysis, 4
in psychodynamic approach, 76
spiritual direction and, 175
spirituality and, 98, 142
SRIs and, 77
in supportive-affective group program, 120

in Vaillant's models, 8
will and, 5–6
Empathy, 10, 60
Empiricism, 98
Engel, George, 9
Enlightenment, 190
Environment, 8, 74
Equanimity, 18
Erikson, Erik, 8
Ethics, 50
Euthanasia, 150
Existential approach
　Havens on, 9
　in "intensive soul care," 120
　paradigm of, 141
　spirituality in, 12, 14
　values in, 10
　will in, 5
Experiential avoidance, 6
"Explanatory pluralism," 22

F

FACIT–Sp, 13–14, 40
Fairness, 95
Faith
　African Americans and, 43
　angst and, 90
　Bonhoeffer on, 90
　commitment and, 15
　components of, 15
　crisis of, 135–137; *See also* Dark Night of the Soul
　definition of, 15
　depression and, 178
　development of, 18–19
　DSM on loss of, 96
　"extrinsic" relationship to, 15–16
　Freud on, 10
　guilt and, 53
　identity and, 15–16
　Kierkegaard on, 89
　personal inadequacy and, 43
　postmodernism and, 22
　treatment and, 100, 144
　trust and, 15
Farber, L.H., 5
Fasting, 16
Faulkner, L.R., 101
Fava, M., 77
Fetzer Institute, 13
Fire, 51
Flexibility, 6
Fluoxetine, 77
Folkman, S., 114
Forgiveness
　in AA, 57
　African Americans and, 43
　Bonhoeffer on, 89–90
　by Christians, 45
　depression and, 35
　guilt and, 58, 91
　hope and, 176
　in Jewish tradition, 45
　maturity and, 19
　for moral failures, 18, 57
　Multidimensional Measurement on, 13
　positive psychology on, 95
　relationships and, 10
　spirituality and, 42
　suicide and, 160, 161
　therapy promoting, 19, 114, 115, 121t, 123–124
　trauma and, 126
　Twelve Step Programs and, 57
Foster, Richard, 48
Four Noble Truths, 15, 49–50
Fowler, James, 18–19
Frankl, Victor, 16, 17, 114
Fredrickson, B.L., 7
Freud, Anna, 91
Freud, Sigmund
　on conflict, 4
　on emotions, 3–4
　on faith, 10
　on psychoanalysis goals, 94
　on religious beliefs, 169

on spirituality, 21
structural theory of the mind, 3
suicide of, 53
on world view, 13n
Freud Versus God (Blazer), 47
Functional Assessment of Chronic Illness Therapy Spiritual Well-Being Scale (FACIT–Sp), 13–14, 40
Fundamentalists, 173
Future Shock (Toffler), 33

G

Gabbard, G.O., 140
Gaby, L., 84
GAF, 8
Gitlin, Todd, 34
Givens, J.L., 42
Global Assessment of Functioning (GAF), 8
Glucocorticoids, 186
Gratitude, 7, 84, 114–116
Greeks, classical, 43–44
Greenspan, M., 60
Greer, S., 114
Grief, 17, 82–86, 98f, 117, 124
Griffith, J.L., 84
Guilt
    altruism and, 60
    over child abuse, 35, 132
    delusional, 58, 74
    depression and, 35–36, 55, 90–91
    diagnosis of, 98f
    Donne on, 35
    faith and, 53
    faith-based communities and, 178
    forgiveness and, 58, 91
    forgiveness-promoting therapy for, 123–124
    insight-oriented psychotherapy for, 132
    self-sacrifice and, 131
    over sexual abuse, 132
    sin and, 17
    societal, 194
    spiritual direction and, 119
    suicide and, 154, 160
    therapist's role in assuaging, 135–137
    trauma and, 80, 125
    of "twice-born," 46
Gutheil, T.G., 140

H

Hallowell, Edward, 34
Hallucinations, 74
Hamilton Depression Rating Scale, 40
Happiness, 23, 94–95, 98f, 177
Harmony, 14
Harvard Study of Adult Development, 8
Havens, L.L., 8
Hayes, S.C., 6
Heal Thyself (Shuman & Meador), 23
Healing Through the Dark Emotions (Greenspan), 60
Herman, Judith, 16, 80
Hindus, 51, 53, 138, 152
Hippocampus, 186–187
"Holy Sonnet III" (Donne), 35
Honesty, 18
Hope
    abuse and, 32, 54, 56, 81, 127
    CBT for, 121t, 122
    demoralization and, 84
    depression and, 31–32, 53, 61, 121t
    despair and, 16, 54
    forgiveness and, 176
    IPT for, 121t, 122
    Multidimensional Measurement on, 13
    Paul's letter to the Romans on, 45
    prayer and, 16
    psychodynamic approach for, 121t
    resiliency and, 115
    spiritual direction for, 121t, 122

spirituality and, 14, 16–17, 20, 56, 121t, 122
suicide and, 153–154, 158–159
Tillich on, 16
trauma and, 122, 125
trust and, 122, 127
world view and, 14, 137
"Horizon of significance," xi
Horowitz, M.J., 82
Horwitz, A.V., 73, 94, 191
How to Win Over Depression (LaHaye), 46
Huguelet, P., 151–152
Humanistic approaches
   to depression, 114–115
   for despair, 133
   identity and, 121t, 122, 130, 133
   perfectionism and, 128
   in Richards' "theistic integrative therapy," 120
   world view and, 138
Humility, 18, 115
Hypothalamic–pituitary–adrenal axis, 186, 187

I

Id, 3–4
Identification, 15
Identity
   in AA, 56, 120
   authority and, 130
   Buddhists on, 15
   depression and, 30–31, 53, 121t
   Erikson's developmental tasks of, 8
   faith and, 15–16
   humanistic approach for, 121t, 122, 130, 133
   Jesus on, 15
   Karp on, 30
   Kierkegaard on, 87
   logotherapy for, 16
   meaning-centered therapy for, 16
   narratives for, 15, 194
   negative, 130–131
   positive psychology and, 130, 133
   self-destructive, 87
   spiritual direction for, 121t, 122
   spirituality and, 14–16, 20, 54, 121t, 122, 176
   suicide and, 157–158
   trauma and, 126
   in Twelve Step Programs, 31, 56, 79, 120
   world view and, 14, 54, 137
Ignatian Exercises, 49, 118, 179
Imagination, 15
Immigrants, pastors of, 173
Insecurity, 81
Insight-oriented psychotherapy, 86, 129, 132
Inspiration, 15
Insurance, x, 170, 175
Integrity, 8, 18, 79, 120, 152
"Intensive soul care," 120
International Conference of the Pontifical Council for Health Care Workers, 49
Interpersonal therapy (IPT)
   for authority issues, 19, 117, 121t, 123
   for bipolar disorder, 75
   for depression, 117–118
   development of, 117
   focus of, 6–7
   for grief, 117
   Havens on, 9
   for hope, 121t, 122
   intimacy and, 19
   for isolation, 37, 121t, 123
   for melancholy, 74
   for perfectionists, 128, 133
   for psychosis, 74
   for rejection, 121t, 123
   for self-sacrificing patients, 133
   spirituality and, 116, 117–118
   world view and, 138
Intimacy, 8, 19, 80

Investment, emotional, 3, 15
IPT; *See* Interpersonal therapy
Islam, adherents of; *See* Muslims
Isolation
  after conflict, 130
  demoralization and, 84, 124
  depression and, 37
  existentialists on, 5
  Gitlin on, 34
  during grief, 124
  IPT for, 37, 121t, 123
  psychodynamic approach for, 121t, 123
  self-sacrifice and, 133
  spiritual direction for, 121t, 123
  spiritually and, 56
  suicide and, 160–161
  trauma and, 125

J

James, William, 46
Jesuits, 49
Jesus
  on despair, 59
  healing by, 45
  historical, 93
  on identity, 15
  prodigal son parable, 19, 161
Jews, 44–45, 112, 152
Jezebel, 44
Job, 44, 127
John of the Cross, St., 45, 61, 91–92
John Paul II, Pope, 49
John Templeton Foundation, 11, 170
Johnson, W.B., 112
Joint Commission, 170
Jones, James, 47–48
Justice, 8, 16, 18

K

Karp, David, 30, 34
Kaye, J., 42

Kendler, K.S., 21, 22, 73
Kierkegaard, Soren, 87–89, 169
Kindness, 7
King, Martin Luther, 15, 176
Kirmayer, L.J., 21
Kirsch, I., 188–189
Kleinman, Arthur, 33, 90
Klerman, G.L., 117
Knowledge, 8, 49, 51, 190
Koenig, Harold, 14, 37–38, 39, 150, 170, 180
Koran, 52; *See also* Qur'an
Kramer, Peter, 77, 185, 191

L

LaHaye, Tim, 46
Larson, David, 38, 170
Lazare, A., 9
Levenson, M.R., 115
Libidinal drives/wishes, 3–4
Life stories, 9, 15
Lincoln, Abraham, 60
Listening to Prozac (Kramer), 185, 191
Living Waters, 48–49, 179, 181
Lizardi, D., 151
Loewenthal, K.M., 52
Logotherapy, 16, 114
Loss of Sadness, The (Horwitz & Wakefield), 191
Love
  depression and, 61
  Hindu path of, 51
  May on, 5
  of the Other, 19
  perfectionism and, 128
  positive psychology on, 7, 95
  prioritization of, 10
  resiliency and, 115
  self-sacrifice for, 131
  spirituality and, 19, 97n, 121t
  in Vaillant's models, 8
  will and, 5
Luhrmann, Tanya, 190–191

M

Ma, S.H., 113
Major depression
  Blazer on origin of, 34
  Buddhists on, 50
  Kendler model for, 73
  Lincoln's response to, 60
  MCBT for, 113
  medications for, 77, 188
  melancholia in, 74
  personality disorders and, 76
  psychosis and, 74
  risk in New England Family Cohort, 41
  spirituality and, 194
Major Depressive Disorder, 72
Malaysia, 39
Malcolm X, 176
Marijuana, 81
Maselko, J., 41
Maslow, Abraham, 114
May, Gerald, 48, 87, 93
May, Rollo, 5, 87
MBCT, 112–114
McCoubrie, R.C., 40
McCullough, M.E., 38
McHugh, P.R., 9
McKinney, W.T., Jr., 72
Meador, K.G., 23, 47
Meaning
  acceptance for, 17
  in Breitbart's group therapy, 114
  cults and, 54–55
  DBT for, 17–18
  demoralization and, 84
  depression and, 33–34, 53, 121t
  FACIT–Sp measurement of, 14, 40
  in Folkman and Greer's approach, 114
  grief and, 17, 83, 85, 124
  in logotherapy, 114
  meditation for, 17, 121t, 122, 176
  mindfulness for, 17, 57, 121t, 122
  Multidimensional Measurement on, 13
  prayer and, 176
  priorities and, 10
  psychological well-being and, 40
  relationships and, 10
  spirituality and, 12, 14, 17–18, 57, 121t, 122
  suicide and, 159
  therapy centered on, 16, 121t, 122, 157
  world view and, 14, 17, 137
Media Unlimited (Gitlin), 34
Medical paradigm, 141
Medication
  AA and, 193
  antidepressants; *See* Antidepressants
  antipsychotics, 74, 190
  apiperazole, 190
  benzodiazepines, 88
  for bipolar disorder, 75
  for depression, 185, 189
  fluoxetine, 77
  Kramer on ethics and, 191
  marketing of, 191, 192
  for melancholia, 74
  oxycodone, 83
  personality disorders and, 77
  vs. prayer, 42, 99
  prescribing of, 190–192
  Prozac, 77
  purpose of, 192
  religious objections to, 135–137, 142, 144, 192–193
  spirituality and, 42, 99–100
Meditation
  in addiction treatment, 18
  benefits of, 113
  in Buddhism, 17, 50
  during dark night of the soul, 92
  in DBT, 17–18
  directed, 118–119
  Jones on, 47
  for meaning, 17, 121t, 122, 176

for mindfulness, 113
pain and, 114
pitfalls, avoiding, 181
secular vs. spiritual, 113–114
sense of purpose and, 121t, 122, 176
stress and, 188
suicide and, 151
Meissner, William, 10
Melancholia, 34, 59, 73, 74, 76, 98f
Miller, D.K., 120
Miller, Lisa, 118
Mindfulness
in addiction treatment, 18
Bergin on, 10
in Buddhism, 17, 50
in CBT, 6
in DBT, 17–18
depression and, 50–51, 170
for meaning, 17, 57, 121t, 122
meditation for, 113
in positive psychology, 95
Richards on, 10
self-transcendence and, 78, 159
sense of purpose and, 17, 121t, 122
Mindfulness-based cognitive therapy (MBCT), 112–114
Miresco, M.J., 21
Monoamine oxidase, 188
Morality
authority and, 18
commitment and, 18
depression and, 35–36, 121t
forgiveness-promoting therapy for, 19, 121t, 123
positive psychology for, 121t, 123
spirituality and, 14, 18–19, 121t, 123
suicide and, 152, 160
world view and, 14, 18, 137
Moreira-Almeida, A., 150
Motivated behavior perspective, 9
Multidimensional Measurement of Religiousness/Spirituality for Use in Health Research, 13

Music, 17, 44, 159
Muslims
CBT for, 112
conflict and, 52
depression and, 38, 39, 52
emotions and, 52
resources for, 173, 174
suicide and, 152
Myth of Sisyphus, The (Camus), 33

N

Nairobi, 178–179
Narratives
for grief, 82–83
for identity, 15, 194
McHugh and Slavney on, 9
in psychodynamic approach, 85
shared societal, 194
spirituality through, 15, 176
for suicidal patients, 157
National Institute on Aging Working Group, *Multidimensional Measurement*, 13
Native Americans, 42, 152
Nausea (Sartre), 33
Neimeyer, R.A., 82, 83
Nelson, C.J., 40
Neuroticism, 77
New Testament, 15, 19, 45–46, 59, 161
Nilsson, K.W., 188
No Exit (Sartre), 33
Noonday Demon, The (Solomon), 72–73
Norepinephrine, 186
Norris, Kathleen, 59, 88
Nucleus accumbens, 186

O

Object relations theory, 10, 116, 123
Objective-descriptive approach, 9
Of Two Minds (Luhrmann), 190–191
Oxycodone, 83

P

Pain, 23, 60, 114
Pargament, K.I., 19, 36, 90, 120, 176–177
Parietal lobe, 187
Parker, G., 73
Patience, 115
Paul, Saint, 45, 46
Peace, sense of, 14, 20, 40, 51
Perfectionism, 128–130, 133
Perry, S.W., 15, 85
Persecution, 20
Personality disorders, 57, 76–78, 98f, 159, 174
Perspective
   dimensional, 9
   disease, 9
   historical, 57
   in MBCT, 113
   motivated behavior, 9
   narratives and, 15
   prayer and, 17
   psychoanalysis and, 191
   rational, 73
   shared, 136
   spirituality and, 142
   Twelve Step Programs and, 20
   worship and, 17
PET, 78
Philosophy, 18
Physical abuse, 32, 81, 126, 187
Pilgrim's Progress (Bunyan), 46
Plato, 21
Pollard, I., 188
Positive psychology
   for depression, 114, 115–116
   for despair, 133
   emotions in, 7
   on forgiveness, 95
   identity and, 130, 133
   integrating, 119–120
   on love, 7, 95
   mindfulness in, 95

   morality and, 121t, 123
   recovery movement and, 2
   resilience development in, 115–116
   spiritual direction and, 120
   themes in, 95
   Vaillant's model based on, 8
Positron emission tomography (PET), 78
Postmodernism, 22, 34
Posttraumatic stress disorder (PTSD), 80
Poverty, 23
Prayer
   African Americans and, 43
   boundaries and, 140–141
   in CBT, 112
   by Christians, 45, 47, 48, 49
   in coping strategy, 43
   during dark night of the soul, 92
   depression and, 57–58
   directed, 118–119
   hope and, 16
   by Jews, 44–45
   Jones on, 47
   meaning and, 176
   vs. medication, 42, 99
   Multidimensional Measurement on, 13
   by Muslims, 39, 52
   perspective and, 17
   recovery and, 39
   self-transcendence and, 159
Predestination, 127
Prefrontal cortex, 186, 187–188
Prigerson, H.G., 82
Priorities, 10
Probst, L.R., 38, 112
Prodigal son parable, 19, 161
Projection, 20
Protestants, 46–47
Prozac, 77
Psalms, 44, 59
Psychoanalysis, 4, 9, 94, 116–117, 191

Psychodynamic approach
  acceptance in, 115
  for authority issues, 121t, 123
  case formulation for, 100–101
  hope and, 121t
  in "intensive soul care," 120
  for isolation, 121t, 123
  narratives in, 85
  objective of, 4
  paradigm of, 141
  on personality disorders, 76
  for rejection, 121t, 123
  spiritual direction and, 176
  spirituality in, 116
  will in, 4
  world view and, 138
Psychology, 12
Psychosis, 73, 74, 75, 98f, 157
PTSD, 80
Purpose, sense of
  acceptance for, 17
  cults and, 54–55
  DBT for, 17–18
  demoralization and, 84
  depression and, 33–34, 60, 121t
  FACIT–Sp measurement of, 14
  in Folkman and Greer's approach, 114
  in logotherapy, 114
  meaning-centered approach for, 121t, 122
  meditation for, 17, 121t, 122, 176
  mindfulness for, 17, 121t, 122
  prayer and, 176
  psychological well-being and, 40
  spirituality and, 14, 17–18, 121t, 122
  suicide and, 159
  world view and, 14, 137
Purpose Driven Life, The (Warren), 176

Q

Qur'an, 39; *See also* Koran

R

Racism, 20
Rasic, D.T., 151
Recovery movement, 2
Red Road, 152
Reductionism, 21–22, 191
Rejection
  after conflict, 130
  demoralization and, 124
  IPT for, 121t, 123
  by the Other, 14, 19, 97n
  perfectionism and, 128
  psychodynamic approach for, 121t, 123
  self-sacrifice and, 131, 133
  spiritual direction for, 121t, 123
  spirituality and, 55
  suicide and, 160–161
Religion
  definition of, 12
  depression and, 38–41
  education and training on, 11
  on moral failures, 18
  Multidimensional Measurement on, 13
  spirituality and, 13
  standards from, 18
  suicide and, 150–152, 160
  survey of U.S. physicians, 11
  World Psychiatric Association on, 11
Repetition compulsion, 176
Repetitive transcranial magnetic stimulation, 189
Resilience, 2, 6, 8
Rethinking Psychiatry (Kleinman), 33
Rheumatoid arthritis, 41–42
Richards, Allan, 10
Richards, S., 120
Rieff, Philip, 191
Rizzuto, Ana-Maria, 10, 116
Romans, Paul's letter to the, 45
Rural congregations, 173

S

Sartre, Jean-Paul, 33, 52–53
Satisfaction, sense of, 20
Saul, King, 44
Schafer, Roy, 4
Schatzberg, A. F., 73
Schizophrenia, 157
Segal, Z.V., 50, 113
Selective serotonin reuptake inhibitors (SSRIs), 188, 189
Self
  Buddhism on, 49–50
  in CBT, 133
  depression and, 50
  grief and, 83
  Kierkegaard on, 87, 89
  relationships with, 10
  soul and, 2
  spirituality and, 176–177, 193
  trauma and, 80, 125
Self-sacrifice, 131–132, 133
Self-transcendence, 17, 24, 42, 77–78, 159, 188
Seligman, Martin, 7, 115–116
Serotonin, 21, 78, 186, 188
Serotonin norepinephrine reuptake inhibitors (SNRIs), 188
Serotonin reuptake inhibitors (SRIs), 77, 78, 188
Sexual abuse, 56, 81, 132, 156, 158, 187
Shafranske, E.P., 116
Shame, 55, 81, 90, 125, 132, 178
Shuman, J.J., 23, 47
Sickness Unto Death, The (Kierkegaard), 87
Sikhs, 152
Sin, 17, 45, 89–90, 178
Slavney, P.R., 9, 84
Sloan, R.P., 23
Smith, T.B., 38
Smoking, 79
Snow, C.P., 190

SNRIs, 188
Social intelligence, 8
Sociology, 12
Solomon, A., 32, 60, 72–73
Southern Medical Association, 170
Speaking of Sadness (Karp), 34
Sperry, L., 118, 119–120
Spirit of the Disciplines, The (Willard), 48
Spiritual direction
  abuse and, 119
  for authority issues, 121t, 123
  awareness in, 118
  for Buddhists, 51
  for Christians, 48
  during dark night of the soul, 48, 124
  description of, 118–119
  education and training on, 175–176
  goal of, 175
  guilt and, 119
  for hope, 121t, 122
  for identity, 121t, 122
  for isolation, 121t, 123
  medication and, 119
  for perfectionists, 128, 133
  pitfalls, avoiding, 175–176, 181
  positive psychology and, 120
  psychodynamic approach and, 176
  for rejection, 121t, 123
  for self-sacrificing patients, 133
  Sperry on, 118
  spirituality and, 20, 116
  world view and, 14, 138
"Spiritual/psychotherapeutic intervention," 120
Spiritual Transcendence Scale, 40
Spiritual Well-Being Scale (SWBS), 40
Spirituality
  agnostics and, 12
  assessment of, 97n, 172
  atheists and, 12
  attuned, 14, 17–18, 97n, 121t, 122

Index 213

  authority and, 14, 19–21, 121t, 123,
     176–177
  awareness and, 58
  bipolar disorder and, 75
  child abuse and, 54, 56, 81, 127,
     132
  constructive, 19–20
  contemplative, 14, 17–18, 97n, 121t,
     122
  definition of, 12
  depression and, 40–43, 53–62, 96,
     141–142
  destructive, 19, 20
  emotions and, 98, 142
  engaged, 14–16, 97n, 121t, 122
  in existential approach, 12, 14
  feeling loved and accepted, 19, 97n,
     121t
  forgiveness and, 42
  Freud on, 21
  hope and, 14, 16–17, 20, 56, 121t,
     122
  identity and, 14–16, 20, 54, 121t,
     122, 176
  integrated, 14, 16, 97n, 121t, 122
  IPT and, 116, 117–118
  isolation and, 56
  love and, 19, 97n, 121t
  major depression and, 194
  mature, 14, 18–19, 97n, 121t
  meaning and, 12, 14, 17–18, 57,
     121t, 122
  medication and, 42, 99–100
  morality and, 14, 18–19, 121t, 123
  Multidimensional Measurement on,
     13
  through narratives, 15, 176
  neurobiology of, 185, 187–188,
     193–194
  outcomes of, 14
  perspective and, 142
  problematic, 19, 20–21
  psychoanalysis and, 116–117
  in psychodynamic approach, 116

  race and, 43
  rejection and, 55
  religion and, 13
  in secular settings, 169–172
  self and, 176–177, 193
  sense of purpose and, 14, 17–18,
     121t, 122
  serotonin and, 78
  spiritual direction and, 20, 116
  suicide and, 20, 151–157, 159, 164
  of therapist, 98–100, 129–130,
     141–143, 171, 180
  transcendence and, 12
  transformative, 15, 121t, 122
  trauma and, 122
  trust and, 56, 177
  in Twelve Step Programs, 134–135
Spirituality Index of Well-Being Scale,
  40
Spiritually oriented psychotherapy
  assessment for, 96–100
  barriers to, 180
  Bergin on, 10
  boundaries in, 136, 137, 140–141
  case formulation for, 100–105
  choice of approach, 121–133, 121t
  confidentiality in, 141
  consent issues in, 136
  countertransference in, 101, 130,
     136, 137, 139, 142
  education and training on, 11,
     181–182
  Engel's biopsychosocial approach
     and, 9, 10
  in faith-based settings, 172–180
  goals of, 134–135
  integrated, 119–133, 169–180,
     193–194
  meditation for, 176
  neurobiology of, 193–194
  objections to, 21–23
  object relations and, 10, 123
  paradigms for, 12, 180

vs. pastoral counseling, 38, 47, 174–175
pitfalls, avoiding, 141–143
priorities in, 124–125
resistance to, x, 143–144, 172
Richards on, 10
in secular settings, 169–172, 181
therapist's role in, 135–137, 172, 180
transference in, 101, 136, 137, 174, 176
World Psychiatric Association on, 11
world view and, 11, 14, 137–140
Splitting, 176
SRIs, 77, 78, 188
SSRIs, 188, 189
Stages of Faith (Fowler), 18–19
Stress, 23, 80, 186–188
Stress diathesis model, 73, 76
Structural theory of the mind, 3
Styron, William, 35, 72–73
Substance abuse
  alcohol, 60, 79, 88
  antidepressants and, 79
  awareness and, 89
  drugs, 60, 79
  neglect during, 90
  pastoral counseling on, 173
  treatment, spiritual assessment in, 170
Suicide
  abuse and, 32, 126–127, 156, 158
  aftermath of, 162–164
  anger and, 160
  assessment of risk for, 97, 98f, 104, 153–156
  atheists and, 52–53
  Buddhists and, 20, 152, 154n
  Camus on, 33, 53
  Christians and, 152
  classical Greek view of, 43–44
  commitment and, 151, 152, 157, 162
  coping strategies and, 152, 156

  demoralization and, 84
  Durkheim on, 33, 150
  forgiveness and, 160, 161
  of Freud, 53
  guilt and, 154, 160
  Hindus and, 152
  hope and, 153–154, 158–159
  identity and, 157–158
  integrity and, 152
  isolation and, 160–161
  Jews and, 152
  meaning and, 159
  meditation and, 151
  morality and, 152, 160
  Muslims and, 152
  rejection and, 160–161
  religion and, 150–152, 160
  religiously motivated, 154–155, 154n
  self-transcendence and, 159
  sense of purpose and, 159
  Sikhs and, 152
  spirituality and, 20, 151–157, 159, 164
  in Switzerland, 151–152
  trauma and, 125, 158
  treatment for, 156–159
  trust and, 158
  in United States, 149
Suicide (Durkheim), 33, 150
Superego, 3
Support-affective group program, 120
Supportive psychotherapy, 58, 93, 115, 129
SWBS, 40
Switzerland, suicide study in, 151–152

T

Tan, S., 112
Taylor, C., xi
Teasdale, J.D., 113
Temperance, 8
Thalamus, 187

"Theistic integrative therapy," 120
Tillich, Paul, 16, 88, 177
Toffler, Alvin, 33
Transcendence, 8, 12, 83; *See also* Self-transcendence
Trauma
    CBT for, 133
    from child abuse, 32, 81, 126, 158
    depression and, 32, 80–81, 125–128
    diagnosis of, 98f
    forgiveness and, 126
    guilt and, 80, 125
    Herman on, 16, 80
    hope and, 122, 125
    identity and, 126
    intimacy and, 80
    isolation and, 125
    Living Waters on, 179
    pastoral counseling for, 174
    PTSD, 80
    religious belief and, 17
    self and, 80, 125
    spirituality and, 122
    suicide and, 125, 158
    trust and, 80
    world view and, 16
Trauma and Recovery (Herman), 16, 80
Treatment; *See also* Twelve Step Programs
    ACT, 6
    assessment for, 96–100, 170–171
    biopsychosocial, 9
    Breitbart's group, 114
    case formulation for, 100–105
    CBT; *See* Cognitive behavioral therapy
    child abuse and, 125
    DBT, 17–18, 78, 159
    dynamic; *See* Psychodynamic approach
    ECT, 74, 154, 188
    Engel on, 9
    existential; *See* Existential approach
    faith and, 100, 144
    flow chart for, 98f
    Folkman and Greer's approach to, 114
    forgiveness-promoting, 19, 114, 115, 121t, 123–124
    Havens' comparison of, 8–9
    humanistic; *See* Humanistic approaches
    insight-oriented, 86, 129, 132
    integrated, 193–194
    IPT; *See* Interpersonal therapy
    Lazare on models in, 9
    logotherapy, 16, 114
    MBCT, 112–114
    McHugh and Slavney on, 9
    meaning-centered, 16, 121t, 122, 157
    neurobiology of, 188–194
    objective-descriptive approach to, 9
    paradigms for, 12, 141, 180
    patient's goals in, 99
    planning for, 97–99
    psychoanalysis, 4, 9, 94, 116–117, 191
    resistance to, 100, 143–144
    spiritual; *See* Spiritually oriented psychotherapy
    spiritual direction; *See* Spiritual direction
    supportive, 58, 93, 115, 129
    "theistic integrative," 120
    therapeutic alliance in, 127
    Vaillant's models of, 8
Tricyclics, 188
Triumph of the Therapeutic, The (Rieff), 191
Trust
    in AA, 177
    after abuse, 32, 56, 158
    betrayal and, 32
    depression and, 61
    despair and, 122
    faith and, 15

hope and, 122, 127
spirituality and, 56, 177
suicide and, 158
in therapeutic relationship, 56
trauma and, 80
Truth, 16
Twelve Step Programs
  AA; *See* Alcoholics Anonymous
  awareness and, 20
  choices in, 114
  first step, 59
  focus of, 79
  forgiveness and, 57
  identity in, 31, 56, 79, 120
  integrity in, 79, 120
  perspective and, 20
  projection and, 20
  referrals to, 136
  satisfaction and, 20
  self-sacrifice and, 132
  spirituality in, 134–135
Tyler, F.B., 179

U

United States
  depression in, ix
  Muslim imams in, 173
  physician's religious beliefs and medical care in, 11
  suicides in, 149

V

Vagal nerve stimulation, 189
Vaillant, George, 1, 8
Vajravaradri, 51
Values, 22
Varieties of Religious Experience, The (James), 46
Varma, S.L., 39
Ventral striatum, 186
Verbal abuse, 32, 124, 126
Viederman, M., 15, 85

Vietnam, 20, 154n
Vineyard Christian Fellowship, 48
Virtues, 57, 95, 114

W

Wachholtz, A.B., 113–114
Wakefield, J.C., 73, 82, 94, 191
Walker, R.L., 151
Warren, Rick, *The Purpose Driven Life*, 176
Water, 51
What Really Matters (Kleinman), 90
Whiffen, V.E., 76
Whites, 43
WHO, 11
Will, 4–6
Willard, Dallas, 48
Wilson, Eric, 59
Wind, 51
Wink, P., 41
Wisdom
  in Buddhism, 50
  CBT and, 144
  Farber on, 5
  Hindu goddess of, 51
  resiliency and, 115
  suicide and, 164
  in Vaillant's models, 8
  world view and, 95
Work, 51
World Health Organization (WHO), 11
World Psychiatric Association, 11
World view
  authority and, 14, 19, 137
  autonomy and, 137
  Blazer on, 34
  CBT and, 138
  courage and, 95
  Freud on, 13n
  grief and, 83
  hope and, 14, 137
  humanistic approaches and, 138

identity and, 14, 54, 137
IPT and, 138
meaning and, 14, 17, 137
morality and, 14, 18, 137
priorities and, 10
in psychodynamic approach, 138
purpose and, 14, 137
spiritual direction and, 14, 138
of therapist, 11, 137–140, 171

trauma and, 16
virtues and, 95
Worship, 16, 17, 23, 57, 159
Worthington, E.L., 115

Y

Yalom, Irving, 5, 87
Yoga, 51